Evitchka

A True Story of Survival, Hope and Love

By Lawrence P. Levitt
and Stephanie Smartschan

Printed in the United States of America

FIRST EDITION

Print ISBN: 978-1-952352-23-2
eBook ISBN: 978-1-952352-24-9

Published by:

Crave Press

www.cravepress.com

We dedicate this book to Eva,
aka Evitchka,
who has inspired us to try to live our lives
the way she lived hers.

THANK YOU FOR HELPING US HONOR EVA'S LEGACY AND SHARE HER INCREDIBLE STORY.

LARRY LEVITT

STEPHANIE SMARTSCHAN

Preface

As I entered my ninth decade of life, I thought that maybe the lessons I had learned — as a physician, a son, a father, a grandfather — would be beneficial to share. But as I sat down to write my story, I realized that my story wasn't really mine. At least, it didn't start with me. Everything I had seen and accomplished and overcome was made possible by the woman who stood by my side for 61 years. And it was, in fact, from her family's bravery and determination that I drew my strength to try and make this world a better place. That's why I decided that these two stories must be intertwined. For if little Evitchka Ritter, born into World War II, hadn't been protected by the people who loved her, there would be no Larry and Eva, and every single thing that I touched, smelled, experienced, would have turned out differently.

Helping me in this effort is Stephanie Smartschan, a writer and editor whom I have admired for a decade. It is our hope that Eva's early years, the remarkable resilience of her beloved parents Olga and Laci (pronounced *Lut-ci*), and the life we went on to live together prove to set an example of courage, perseverance, and selflessness which might influence others in their own lives.

— Larry

Prologue

November 1944

Olga sat wearily on a wooden bench, exhausted to the bone. Her calves ached, and the air was turning colder as the sun began to set. Still, she knew she couldn't rest long. Her only option was to keep moving.

From her perch on the bench, Olga could see a small farmhouse just down the road. Smoke rose from the chimney and a light flickered in the window. Olga squinted and looked again. There were two wooden rocking chairs on the front porch and what looked to be a tricycle abandoned near the entrance to the gate.

Before Olga could assess further, her pretty Evitchka, who had been lulled to sleep by the jostling of her pram and awoken at the stop, let out a little whimper.

"Shh shh," she told her. "I know he'll come for us soon."

Olga pulled out her water canister and screwed off the lid. Tilting Evitchka's little head back, Olga poured the last drops of water down Evitchka's dry throat.

It wouldn't be much longer, Olga knew. She was sure of it. Geza had never let her down before, and she knew that Klara would send him to look for her as soon as he returned from his business trip.

But in the emptiness, how was she to know what became of Geza? The Gendarmes could be knocking at his door this very moment, demanding to see his papers. They surely had found out about the Jewish woman — her sister-in-law — posing as his maid.

She looked down at the little blond-haired, green-eyed toddler at her feet. This was nowhere near the life Olga had imagined for her. Evitchka, her surprise baby, her ray of sunshine, deserved more than a life spent in hiding.

The door to the farmhouse opened. A woman who looked to be about Olga's age stepped out onto the porch and sat down in one of the chairs. She sat quietly for a few minutes, breathing in the cool late fall air. Then came a wail of "Anu" in the distance, and the woman's peaceful moment was over. She stood and returned to the house, the screen door slamming behind her.

Perhaps the answer was right there in front of Olga. Her parents, her husband, they were all but gone. What little family that remained were deep in hiding, spread to the four winds. If something happened to her...she couldn't even think about it.

Olga looked down again at the child, her eyelids now fluttering as she drifted off again.

If she waited until dark, she could easily make her way to the farmhouse without being spotted. She could knock on the door and then disappear into the night. A better life for her pretty Evitchka.

Olga looked up just as a few tiny snowflakes floated from the sky. She stretched out her arm to catch them on the back of her hand. Then, she wearily gripped the handles of the pram and trudged on.

PART 1

1

March 22, 1939

The waitress delivered a steaming cup of tea, and Olga thanked her profusely. The excitement of the last week had left her feeling anxious, and she tried her hardest to relax as she settled in for her first café lunch as a married woman.

"By this afternoon, we'll be breathing in the mountain air, just the two of us," her new husband assured her, reaching across the table to take her hand as she placed the teacup in its saucer.

"I can't believe our wedding was only yesterday," Olga said wistfully. "Oh how I wish all of our family could have been there."

"We did the best we could under the circumstances," her husband assured her once again. "Besides, you looked so beautiful in that dress your mother made standing under the *chuppah*, and now you are officially Mrs. Leopold Ritter." He beamed and kissed her hand adoringly.

Though he didn't dare voice his thoughts out loud, Leopold — known to his friends and family as Laci — also wished desperately that they could have gone through with the reception they had planned — the one where a decadent meal would have been served and a band would have played late into the night.

Tensions had simmered for months as they cautiously approached their big day, but then, a week ago, those tensions rose to a boil. The country they'd lived in – Czechoslovakia – no longer existed. The Nazi-aligned Slovak State had declared independence on March 14, with the Germans promising protection from Hungary, which lay to the southeast and eyed additional territorial gains. The new Slovak State contained the city of Prešov where their wedding was supposed to take place and where they now sat, as well as their hometown of Humenné, sixty kilometers east.

Two days later, Nazi troops occupied Czech lands to the west, declaring them to the Protectorate of Bohemia and Moravia.

It was clear that the spectacle of a lavish party would not have been prudent on their wedding day scheduled for March 21, 1939, so they gave up the social hall in place of a small ceremony closer to home.

"I'm glad we decided to keep the plans for our honeymoon," said Olga, interrupting his thoughts.

"Only another hour or so on the train until we get to our hotel," he assured her. The Tatra Mountains, a popular destination for newlyweds, lay to the northwest, on the Polish border.

As they talked about the week ahead and waited for their food to arrive, two men entered the small café and sat down in the booth behind them. Glancing over her shoulder, Olga noticed the men never took off their coats. With her back to them, she could just barely make out the words as they spoke to each other in a harsh whisper. Whatever they were discussing, the urgency in their voices was apparent.

Then she heard a word that made her heart skip a beat: "Humenné."

Olga thought immediately of her parents. She would never forgive herself if something happened to them. She stood up quickly, her hands now shaking.

"Laci, we need to go home, now," she implored.

"Of course," he agreed, grabbing his coat and tossing a few coins on the table without so much as a question. "Let's see if we can find a taxi."

They walked out of the café and onto the main street, hand in hand and carting their luggage behind them.

They attracted the attention of a handful of drivers, but each one refused the fare when he learned of their intended destination. At last, they found a driver willing to take the risk — for a price.

"One thousand crowns," the driver demanded.

Laci reached into his pocket for his wallet and handed over the cash. They navigated checkpoints in nearly every town they approached, and the drive which should have taken an hour lasted several. Each checkpoint was more trouble than the one before, and they were thankful for their driver who skillfully convinced each guard to let them pass.

When they finally reached their town, they were relieved to find the streets calm. They pulled up to the house — Olga's childhood home and Laci's new one — gathered their bags, slammed the doors of the taxi shut, and rushed inside.

Their dog, Rexi, barked excitedly, running over to sniff their coats.

"Anu, Apu," Olga called urgently.

Morris and Anna Roth hurried to the entryway to greet them. "What are you doing here?" Morris asked. "What's all this excitement about?"

Laci explained what they had overheard and what led them to opt out of their honeymoon before it had even begun.

Morris sighed. He had tried to remain optimistic, to project strength so that his only daughter could enjoy a peaceful and happy start to her marriage. He should have realized, with the events of the past week, that this was just not to be.

"I'm glad you're here and that you're safe," he said, pulling Olga in for an embrace.

The next day, war indeed broke out between the Hungarians and the Slovaks. After a sudden attack and clear intentions to move west, Hungarian troops advanced quickly into eastern Slovak territory which surprised both the Slovaks and Germany. The Slovaks were also surprised to find that Germany did not, in fact, come to their aid as promised. After about a week of fighting, the Hungarian army proved to be too large and cohesive. The Slovaks were forced to cede another strip of eastern Slovak territory to Hungary.

What remained of Slovak territory quickly began to echo the policies of the German government, and the anti-Jewish sentiment that came with it. Not long after Laci and Olga returned from their would-be honeymoon, there came a knock at the door just as the family sat down for dinner.

They had heard a local police officer was killed and that the police were looking for Jews to blame, so were not all that surprised to see two officers standing at the door. The family had a good rapport with much of the local police force, but these were officers they didn't recognize.

The officers pushed their way in without a word, and one headed straight up the stairs, right into Laci and Olga's bedroom, while the other stood guard at the door. Minutes later, the upstairs officer emerged holding a gold bracelet. Taking this as evidence of their guilt — for what, they weren't sure — the officers told Laci and Morris they were under arrest.

Laci looked forlornly at his new wife as they were led away to the officers' car.

Had they taken the men to a jail in Humenné, they might have been able to talk their way out of the situation. They knew people, had friends there. Instead, the men were driven about an hour away to a crowded jail in Prešov.

They were allowed to bring in food, but Laci couldn't eat. He became violently ill, perhaps a bug he caught in the putrid conditions. After about a week, he couldn't take it anymore. He found the friendliest looking officer and asked for his help. The man indeed agreed to help, to let Laci and Morris go — as long as they paid him fifty thousand crowns. Though Laci knew he could buy a house with that kind of money, he had no choice but to agree. The officer rode with Laci and Morris in a taxi back to Humenné, straight to the bank, where Morris handed over the money before they were set free.

It wouldn't be for long. Four weeks later, dinner was once again interrupted and Laci again taken to jail, this time for reportedly exchanging money for American dollars. He was taken to a different jail this time, but he now had a handle on the system. He paid his way out the very same night.

2

January 1941

Laci looked up from his desk, startled at the sound of the swinging door banging shut against the wooden post. He could hear the wind whistling in the distance.

He had his nose to the grindstone all morning, buried deep in the company books, opening the mail, filling out paperwork. On most days, he liked to get out of the office and walk the yard, but today there was no time.

His brother Jack walked in, slowly unraveling the icy scarf from around his neck.

"Finished up the order, truck's all loaded," Jack said, stomping loudly as he wiped the bits of snow and mud off his worn boots.

"Good, because three more orders just came in," Laci told him.

Since Germany had invaded Poland with the support of the Slovak army, about six months after his marriage to Olga, lumber orders had gone through the roof. They knew the Germans were using their lumber to make railroad ties. They also knew that the value the Germans placed on their lumber was the only insurance policy they had to keep their families from being deported, and so they kept working.

They were doing everything they could to keep up with demand. Most Sundays included a trip to the yard to tie up one loose end or another. But they never worked long hours on Fridays. They left that to Hanz Grafinger, who on paper had become their boss since, as Jews, they had lost the right to own a business.

Glancing out of the half-fogged window, Laci could see the bright sun still shining over the lumber yard. Even though it was just past mid-day, it was time for them to finish up if they wanted to make it home before the early winter sunset.

"We better get going. Olga won't stand for it if we're late," he said, rising with a slight creak in his knees and turning around to grab his coat from the rack.

Laci leaned back over his desk to scribble one more note in his ledger, and then he closed the book. He examined his calloused hands for a moment before pulling on his woolen gloves.

Jack grabbed the briefcase he had stuffed in the corner earlier that day. He gave his scarf a shake before wrapping it around his neck again.

They stepped out into the cool air. Flurries began to fall as Jack locked the office door, and the two brothers set off for the train, waving jovially to their hard-working employees as they left the yard.

Leopold and Jack Ritter took over the family business when their father Moshe got sick. Moshe had started the lumber business in the small village of Radvan in the late 1800s to support his wife and their five children. At the time, the village was part of Hungary.

He invested what little he had to buy that first track of forest land. Then he cut down the trees and sold the lumber to builders working on houses and railroad ties. With his profits, he was able to keep buying land and repeating the process. Soon, he added on the production of charcoal from burning his wood, which he was able to sell to countries like Switzerland and Italy at a nice profit. They lived a comfortable life as the children grew.

When he lost his wife Regina to tuberculosis, Moshe was devastated. Still, he kept working, saw his children into early adulthood, and found a way to start over.

When Moshe met Eugenia, the twenty-year age gap didn't faze him. She wanted to have children and start a family of her own. Over a decade, five more children were born to Moshe and Eugenia: Regina, named for his first wife, Leopold, Jack, Julia, and Munci. By the time Munci came into the picture, Moshe was fifty-nine years old and ready to retire. But he knew he needed to hang on until his sons were ready to take over the business.

Moshe worked long hours as Laci and Jack attended school in the nearby town of Humenné, practically cosmopolitan compared to Radvan. However, Radvan was particularly picturesque — a kilometer and a half at its widest, with about one hundred and fifty families calling it home. The families came from all different backgrounds, yet they enjoyed a neighborly camaraderie.

The Ritters lived on Radvan's main street, bottling milk from their two cows — only ever milked by the maid — and collecting eggs from their chicken coop. The small village had somehow become the regional center of Jewish life, with its twenty-five Jewish families, and many more traveling in on Fridays and Saturdays to attend synagogue and use the local mikvah, a ritual bathhouse.

On Shabbat and Jewish holidays, families from afar would gather at the Ritter house in Radvan, where Yiddish words rang out, cousins played in the nearby fields, and the brisket melted in your mouth.

Before World War I, Laci and Jack attended a Hungarian school, but after the war, when the Austria-Hungary empire collapsed and Czechoslovakia declared its independence, they found themselves at a Czechoslovak high school. That didn't last long, however, as Moshe became unable to keep up with the lumber yard and his sons spent more and more time by his side.

By this time, their lumber yard was the largest employer in town, with more than two hundred men of all backgrounds on the payroll. Laci and Jack's new responsibilities included traveling to support the business.

Laci's travels took him across the country and outside of it. On one occasion, he stayed on the same floor of a Budapest hotel where the king of Hungary would stay. In 1934, he found himself on business in Vienna, delivering wood for a paper factory, when Engelbert Dollfuss, an Austrian politician who had tried to suppress the socialist movement, was assassinated by Nazi agents as part of a failed coup attempt. Laci watched his funeral procession from the windows of the Bristol Hotel.

It was nearing 3:00 when Laci and Jack boarded the train car for the fourteen-mile ride south to Humenné. Laci settled into a seat against a window, and as the train chugged over the tracks, he paged through the copy of the *Slovak Record* he had picked up at the station. He saw headlines like, "Mussolini consents to German troops entering Italy," and, "Bulgaria passes law for the 'protection of the nation.'"

It's not that the headlines were coming as a shock at this point. He had watched for the better part of three years as Hitler's troubling policies in Germany spilled over like a slow-moving tidal wave.

For the Jews in Radvan and Humenné, that meant increasing restrictions. They couldn't shop at the market before 10:00 in the morning, they were not allowed to occupy rooms facing the front of the street, and they were not able to own a radio or have a maid under sixty years old. Most upsetting for him, however, was they couldn't own businesses. So he had hired Grafinger, a German man who worked in his wife's uncle's engineering shop, to run his lumber yard. The arrangement was in name only, of course, and everybody knew it.

By paying Grafinger, Laci was able to hold onto what his father had built, and what he and his family counted on for their livelihood. Best for him to focus on the tasks in front of him: manage the payroll, fill the orders, and keep his customers happy.

Weary from the train ride and feeling heavy from the day's news, Laci felt his burden lighten as he stepped into the modest yet comfortable home attached to a vinegar factory where he lived with Olga and her parents.

The smell of chicken soup simmering on the stove fused with the familiar fragrance of fresh challah browning in the oven. Their housekeeper, Marcha, must have already finished stuffing the goose. She breezed by with hands full of silverware as she headed toward the dining room to set the table.

Laci gave Olga a kiss on the cheek before setting down his briefcase and pulling off his coat and gloves.

His mother-in-law Anna busied herself in the kitchen, giving the soup a stir. He knew his father-in-law would also be closing up shop shortly in the vinegar factory. Laci would always associate the pungent smell of vinegar with Morris Roth.

Laci knew the Roths had absolutely not wanted their only daughter to marry a lumberer from Radvan. Wasn't it his luck to run into her during one of his business trips to Humenné, and he had the good sense to ask her out to boot. On that first night he picked her up, he remembered the worried looks her parents shared over the dirt under his fingernails and his heavily scuffed boots.

But he had grown on them, eventually joining them for frequent dinners and then, some months later, asking Morris for his daughter's hand in marriage.

Laci couldn't have been more relieved when Morris gave his blessing, especially knowing how protective Morris was over Olga. Morris had lost Olga's brother, his only son, to rheumatic fever at age seven. Olga was his everything.

Along with his blessing, Morris also gave Laci a precious gold watch that had been a family heirloom. Laci treasured that watch and wore it wherever he went until not long after their engagement, while on a business trip to Kežmarok to deliver lumber late in 1938, he found himself caught up in a raid. He was taken to the nearby police station where guards greedily removed the watch from his wrist. He was released the next morning, but the knot that had formed in the pit of his stomach refused to be released. This was a harbinger of things to come, he feared.

Upon returning home, downtrodden, he recounted the story to his wife and future in-laws. Forget the watch, they said. We're just glad you're home safely.

But he couldn't, and after he told the same story to a Hlinka guard with whom he was friendly, he was surprised when, a few days later, the guard called him up and asked him to come to the station. When he arrived, there on the man's desk was his gold watch.

How lucky, Laci thought, looking down at that same watch and noting the time. It was almost sundown. Anna pulled the window shades closed and took off her apron. They all made their way to the dining room.

The two couples gathered around the Roth family's prized candelabra, its freshly polished silver nearly glimmering thanks to

Marcha. While tradition called for the lighting of two candles on Shabbat, this family heirloom held five.

A slim white candle stood tall in the center, surrounded by a candle at each corner waiting to be lit. With the others leaning close, Anna lit the match and set the center candle aflame before bathing it in light from each direction. She covered her eyes and recited, *"Baruch atah Adonai, Eloheinu Melech haolam, asher kid'shanu b'mitzvotav v'zivanu l'hadlik ner shel Shabbat."*

Then it was Morris's turn to say the blessings over the wine and challah. "Good Shabbos," he rejoiced afterward, kissing his wife and daughter and then offering Laci a genial hug.

They savored the meal as always, the matzah balls light and fluffy, the goose flavorful and tender. Afterward, they enjoyed homemade chocolate babka. They would save Anna's special coffee cake for the morning.

3

January 1942

In the year that followed, the Ritters and Roths became adept at figuring out how to skirt the new laws that kept popping up. When they were told they could no longer occupy rooms facing the street, they rented their front rooms to two Christians who gave them no trouble. Laci even purchased a radio for the men, and they allowed him to listen with them so he could find out what was going on across and outside of the country.

Then in early 1942, two consequential events would considerably raise the stakes for their family.

The first was a happy occasion, albeit a surprising one. With the world around them in disarray, starting a family had not seemed advisable, and they had planned to wait until the worst had passed. Nevertheless, on January 12, 1942, little Evitchka was born.

This green-eyed cherub was the pride of her family, the only child of her parents, and the only grandchild of her grandparents on her mother's side. She was the light in an otherwise darkening world, and they soaked up her very being.

Her parents dressed her in the finest clothes, traveling to Košice or Prague to procure them. Olga felt more at ease than she had in years as she sang songs from her childhood and nuzzled her darling daughter to her breast.

Sadly, they couldn't relax in newborn bliss for long. Two months later, the deportations began.

The Slovak police began rounding up the local Jews, handing them over to the Germans for transport.

Laci and Jack were very fortunate that their lumber business was considered to be essential. The two men and their families were given an exemption because of this. Morris and Anna Roth also received such an exemption for Morris's work in the vinegar factory.

Jack had married his wife Roszi two years after Laci and Olga had wed. They hunkered down with their own newborn daughter Judy, born six weeks after Evitchka, and hoped the worst would pass as Jack continued working.

Laci and Jack's little sister, Munci, was not so lucky. Munci was still living in Radvan when the police invaded the town and picked up all the single Jewish boys and girls. News traveled fast, and Laci quickly caught wind that his sister had been taken to the local jail. He rushed to the police headquarters in Radvan and found the head of the Gendarme, who happened to be an old friend.

"Please, can you help her?" he begged his friend, the officer.

"There's nothing I can do," the officer said. "This is the law."

"There has to be something you can do," he continued to beg. "There's no reason for her to stay here on the floor with so many people. Let me take her home, and I give you my word that I will bring her to the railroad station tomorrow morning."

The officer reluctantly agreed, and Laci did keep to his word, in fear for his own family, bringing his sister in the next day. His eyes filled with tears as he watched the train full of the children of his youth leave the station. It was mere moments before he regretted his decision to turn his sister over.

He ran outside to hail a taxi, ordering the driver to follow the transport to the next station. He got there in time to see a train of Jewish girls and boys being unloaded.

The train emptied, but there was no sign of his sister. A second transport pulled in and emptied; still no sign of her. He had nearly given up when a third train pulled into the station. He saw his friend from the Gendarme waiting outside one of the doors. This time, he approached the man and made him an offer without hesitation.

"I will try," his friend said, taking the money from Laci's hands, "but I can't make any promises."

He waited nervously, shifting from one foot to the other. Then, his eyes filled with tears again as he saw, among the throngs of solemn-faced teenagers and young adults, his sister disembark. He watched as the officer approached her and whispered something in her ear. She nodded, then continued to move with the flow of the crowd toward the station. Just as she neared the doors, he watched her veer off and head in his direction. None of the other busy officers paid her any mind.

"I'm so sorry," Laci said, the tears now freely flowing as he ushered her into the waiting taxi. Shaken, Munci remained silent for the entire ride back to Radvan. It was only later that they learned that Munci was the only one of the two hundred youth to be released. This group of young people would go on to be among the first to arrive at, and be forced to build, a camp for Jews that came to be known as Auschwitz.

When Munci returned to Radvan, Laci hired her on at the lumber factory, giving her some protection as an essential worker. She didn't have the official exemptions of her brothers, but the local police were friendly.

When word spread soon after that the Gestapo were coming to search the village, Munci knew she had to disappear. A friendly employee of the lumber yard and his family let her hide in their attic. They brought her food and took care of her. Her parents were hiding in the same family's basement. Days later, the worst blew over, and they were able to emerge from their hiding places.

Then, a few weeks later, the local police tipped them off that the Gestapo were returning again. This time, she hid with her parents in a cellar, sleeping on potato sacks for almost a week. Moshe, an old man by that time, couldn't take it. During the first World War, people were nice to him, and he couldn't understand why he had to hide. He didn't do anything to anybody, he thought. But the rest of the family knew that they had to endure it if they wanted to live, and they convinced him to stay in hiding.

In 1943 came a new law that a German was not allowed to have a Jew employed. By that time, the lumber yard was officially owned by a German, Grafinger.

Laci was sitting at his kitchen table in Humenné one Sunday afternoon the following January when a friend from city hall came by to tell him the news.

"You need to disappear," he told Laci.

Laci looked out the window, and couldn't help but smile as he watched his pretty little Evitchka, who had just turned two years old, being pulled around in the snow by their dog Rexi. The sound of her giggle carried through the winter air and lightened his heart.

Just as quickly, the heaviness returned and he stood up from the table. "I understand," he told his friend.

He went outside to find Olga, whose eyes were filled with pure love and adoration as she witnessed Evitchka's glee.

He told her what he had just learned and watched the expression on her face quickly turn to worry. "We need to hide," she said firmly.

With no time to plan, Olga hurried over to pick up her cold and happy child. "We're going on a visit," she cooed.

Together, the family of three walked across the street to the home of a friendly neighbor and explained the situation. The neighbor agreed to take them in, ushering them inside and closing the door behind them.

Olga's parents would be okay, they thought. Their "boss" was a Slovak.

Sure enough, an hour later, Laci peered through the window of his neighbor's house and saw two Gendarmes knocking on his door. Marcha answered, and Laci watched as she spoke to the men, but he couldn't make out what they were saying. No, he isn't here, Laci assumed. After a minute or two, the officers turned around and left.

The Gendarmes tasked with enforcing the new rule were Slovak, he knew, and this was a German law. They may not have looked too hard this time, but he knew in his heart that this wouldn't be the end of it.

As soon as they left, Laci sprang into action. He had to look for a new "boss." And he had to make sure his wife and daughter were safe.

They quickly made arrangements for Olga and Evitchka to travel to Hungary, where Olga had an aunt living on a big estate in Debrecen. It pained him deeply to say goodbye to the two people he loved more than anything in the world, but he couldn't risk that the officers would return and put them all on the next transport.

He couldn't have been more thankful when he learned that Olga and Evitchka had arrived safely. For two months, they wrote letters to each other, and Laci felt like this arrangement could be a lasting one. That all changed on March 19, 1944, however, when German forces occupied Hungary.

Soon Hungarian authorities began ordering Jews living outside of Budapest to concentrate in certain cities. Hungarian Gendarmes were sent into the rural regions to round up the Jews and dispatch them to these so-called ghettos. By April, the Gendarmes had arrived in Debrecen, and Olga knew she would no longer be safe there.

She wrote to Laci to tell him the news, and together they hatched a plan for Olga and Evitchka to return home.

First, Olga went to a local doctor who was friendly with her aunt. He gave her a certificate saying she needed an operation for a fibroid tumor. It was true, in fact, that she did need the operation, but this was something she had known for months. Jews weren't allowed to travel by rail at that time, but the certificate gave her passage to get on a train with her cousin and young daughter.

"Remember, if we meet anyone and they ask your name, tell them it's 'Pretty Evitchka,'" Olga reminded her toddler, stroking the child's hair. She needn't worry; little Evitchka had no idea her last name was Ritter anyway. They had never told her, as the name was easily recognized for its German Jewish origins.

When they reached the train station, they were met by a Hungarian woman that Laci had hired to transport them the rest of the way to the Slovak border.

They drove through the night, the two women and young child crouched low in the back seat, covered by blankets.

They reached the border, thanked their driver, and were led by peasants to a hidden path in the woods where they were to cross. Suddenly they heard a loud voice shout, "Stop!" and knew they had been caught. But then Olga heard the sounds of the guards speaking Czech to the peasants and was quickly relieved. The Czechs you could pay off. The Hungarians wanted Jewish blood and, in her experience, were as vicious as the Germans themselves.

She handed over the cash her husband had sent for just this occasion. The guards waved her through and, by morning, Olga and Evitchka pulled up in front of their home in Humenné. It felt to Olga as if it had been years. Or that they had never left.

Olga was overjoyed to see her husband and parents, and Evitchka bounced right into her father's waiting arms.

Laci's recruitment of a new Slovak boss had kept the Gendarmes off his tail for the time being. They would be able to wait this out, they thought.

4

April 1944

The Germans could feel they were losing the war, which only served to make them more desperate and more dangerous. Munci Ritter knew her days of hiding out in cellars in Radvan with her aging parents were coming to an end. She wouldn't be able to protect them on her own much longer. It was time for them to separate.

She turned to her brother Laci for help, and they were able to secure a place for their parents in a home for older Jews for which they paid a hefty sum on the tacit promise that the residents would remain untouched.

On her own, Munci would have a better chance of blending in. When a friendly police officer came to her door one day in April and told her it was time to get out of town, she was ready. She had been preparing for this day for years, attending church on Sundays and learning all the prayers. She was ready to become Maria Vallaly, born in Brestov, a pretty Christian girl, according to her papers.

She traveled west, to the home of a family recommended by a friend. They took her in and installed her as their housekeeper. In the mornings, she would work in the house, and in the afternoons, they taught her to sew so she could assist them in their tailoring business.

In the evenings, she wrote letters to her parents under false names. "How desperately I miss you," she wrote to them, her tears staining the notepaper. By August, her heart sick from longing and worry, she knew she had to go see them.

She wrote to Laci of her plans, and a reply arrived quickly that she was not, under any circumstances, to make the trip. "You'll be caught and taken to Auschwitz. Please reconsider," he pleaded with her.

"I don't care," she wrote back. "I'm going."

And so, she made arrangements, gathered her false papers, and made the eight-hour trek by train back to Radvan.

Her parents were overjoyed to see their youngest daughter, wrapping her in the tight hugs she had been dreaming of for the last five months and then ushering her inside.

Huddled in their room, they spoke in hushed tones as Munci filled them in on her exploits, and they told her the little they knew of the happenings in Radvan.

Too quickly, it was time for Munci to gather herself for the long journey back. As she bent to kiss her goodbye, Eugenia pulled Munci's face close and held it in her hands.

"I don't think I'm ever going to see you again, my dear Munci," Eugenia said, the tears welling in her eyes.

"No, please, don't say that. This will all be over soon, and we'll be together again," Munci pleaded.

But her mother ignored her and continued. "Don't forget who you are," she said as forcefully as she dared, her fingers moving toward the gold cross that Munci now wore around her neck. "Keep kosher. Light candles on Friday nights. I ask that you do that for me."

Munci nodded wordlessly, tears now streaming from her face, too. She wanted so badly to wish the truth away.

"You'll be safe here," she insisted.

But her mother was right. That was indeed the last time she ever saw her parents.

Olga became pregnant again not long after her return from Hungary. As much as she longed for another child, she knew that this wasn't good news. Her doctor had warned her, for her own health, not to get pregnant with the fibroid tumor intact in her uterus. It was time to have it removed.

With her husband by her side, Olga paid a visit to the best doctor she knew of in the country. That doctor, a German man, told her she needed to have surgery right away.

He removed the tumor and terminated the pregnancy. After a few days, she was released from the hospital and went home to fully recover.

As she convalesced and looked after her Evitchka the best she could, it was clear that the situation around her was only getting worse.

After the first wave of transports in the months after Evitchka's birth, the Jews who remained in Humenné and its surrounding cities had, it seemed, teetered on the edge of stability for the past two years. She had no idea what had become of her friends and neighbors who had all but disappeared, but she also knew it best not to ask questions.

That changed in April of that year, when word quickly spread that two Slovak Jews had escaped from a concentration camp called Auschwitz. The accounts that came from Alfred Wetzler and Walter Rosenberg, who had been assigned to work as scribes for the Nazis, giving them access to reports on the Jews who were being killed there, were chilling.

Then in June, Laci returned from a trip to Bratislava with news that shook the family to its core.

"They're saying the whole region must be freed of Jews," he told his wife and her parents, trying as best he could to hide the panic in his voice.

They all knew that, alas, after all of the exemptions and the luck and the payoffs, it was time for them to leave their home.

Laci went to a friend to inquire about having false papers prepared. Another friend, whose father was a Greek Orthodox minister, presented them with certificates of baptism.

Laci, under the pretense of his new Slovak boss, could leave Humenné and continue to travel for work in cities where Jews were still permitted. After a call to the vinegar factory headquarters in Bratislava, Morris Roth was assigned to a new post in Nitra, and while Laci traveled, Olga thought it best for her and Evitchka to stay with her parents.

Jack would head west with his family and hope the countryside would offer some protection. Munci already had her papers and was working as a maid outside of the county, hiding in plain sight.

They did their best to secure the house and get their affairs in order. They packed up their clothes and some basic furniture, to be loaded onto a cattle car for their new apartment in Nitra. Some of their more precious possessions, however, they decided to leave behind, with the hopes that one day they would return and see them again.

Before departing, the family gathered in the backyard with their most treasured family heirlooms and a shovel. Evitchka, nearly two-and-a-half, played around in the grass while Laci dug a wide, deep hole. Together, Anna and Olga placed their cherished silver candelabra into the ground, its branches covered in dirt. They made a mental note of where they had hidden it.

"This is really happening?" Olga asked her husband, her disbelief paramount.

"We'll be okay," Laci said, grabbing onto her hand. "We'll be back for it."

They traveled west, eight hours or so by train until they reached the city of Nitra. There, they made do in their apartment for a good few months. The jobs that Morris and Laci held were still considered essential, which kept them free from any trouble. Evitchka was becoming more precocious by the minute. Still, they felt like strangers in a strange land and missed their home desperately.

As spring turned to summer, they heard rumors of a movement underfoot to resist the German troops that had occupied Slovak territory and overthrow the Slovak government. By the summer, fighting had broken out in the north-central mountains. Unable to quell the uprising on their own, Slovak authorities invited the help of more German troops. Along with those troops came a unit of the security police that everyone knew had one responsibility — round up and kill Jews.

And by September, the worst news of all — there would be no more exemptions.

5

September 1944

As heartbreaking as it was to think about, Laci knew they would all have a better chance of survival if they split up.

First, they secured a hiding place in Nitra for Morris and Anna through a friend from the vinegar factory. Laci would also stay in Nitra, he decided, and find his own place to hide. But how could he ensure that Olga and Evitchka would be safe?

As they made preparations, Laci remembered the passing offer of a long-time friend of the family, a dear classmate of Olga's from high school. If you find yourself in trouble, Geza Hajtas had told him on a visit to his Bratislava home years ago, you come to me. Reluctantly, Laci felt that time had come.

He could accompany them, of course, but Olga and Evitchka would be safer without him as there was no way to prove they were Jewish like there was for him.

In their final days together, Laci spent as much time as he could with his little daughter, bouncing her on his knee and singing songs to pass the time, trying to soak up every moment.

Then, it was time. Olga hugged her parents fiercely, urging them to stay out of sight and heed any warnings. Reluctantly, she picked up her small suitcase as Laci scooped Evitchka into his arms, and they headed for the train station.

But when they arrived at the station, they immediately knew there was a problem. SS guards were milling about, and loud announcements over the speakers pronounced that no trains would be running that day.

Olga gave her husband a frightened look and gripped Evitchka tightly.

"Let's go," Laci said as calmly as he could.

They picked up their bags and headed back toward the exit. As they weaved their way through the crowd, they heard murmurings — all trains were being stopped so the Jews couldn't flee.

As they neared the doors, Evitchka broke into a coughing fit, evoking stares from the people around them. Hoping desperately not to attract the attention of the guards, Olga and Laci ducked their heads and blended in as best they could as they made their way outside and waited in the long line for a taxi.

"Please take us to the nearest hotel," Laci told the driver breathlessly as they settled into the backseat.

They rode on for about ten minutes until they pulled up to a rundown hotel. Laci asked the driver to wait for a minute as they all got out of the cab.

"You and Evitchka check into a room," Laci said. "Use your false papers."

"But Laci," she pleaded, "can't you just stay with us? Please, just for the night?" The thought of taking on the sole responsibility of keeping their young daughter safe had her starting to panic. She so badly wanted to keep her family together, but she knew deep down that Laci's mind was made up.

"We'll be safer apart," he assured her.

Laci gave his wife a tearful kiss, tousled his daughter's blond hair, and, with one last look back, got into the cab and rode away.

Olga held back her own tears as best she could before entering the small lobby and approaching the front desk. She was on her own now. She gripped her false papers tightly in one hand and held Evitchka's hand in the other.

"One room please," she told the clerk, holding out her papers.

The clerk looked down at the papers, then up at her suspiciously. She held her breath, fidgeting around and unable to look him in the eye. After a minute or so of examining the papers, he handed her a key.

"Room five, out to the left," he said.

She thanked him and made her way the short distance to the door marked "five." Once inside, she pulled out a snack for Evitchka that she had packed in her bag and approached the dingy bathroom mirror, splashing water on her tired face.

Evitchka finished her snack and then started to cry. This wasn't like her Evitchka, who was usually as calm and jovial as a toddler can be. She knew right away that something must be wrong. She picked up her daughter and now, really looking at her, noted the rosy cheeks and pale complexion that the events of the day had led her to miss. She put her lips to the little girl's forehead. It felt warm.

She drew the child into her lap and stroked the back of her head, bouncing her up and down gently to soothe the crying. Evitchka had finally settled and was just drifting off when Olga heard a loud pounding at the door.

"*Razzia!*" she heard a loud voice call. A raid.

Her breath quickened and she started to feel faint. What should she do? She could hide, but she had a feeling the officer already knew she was in there. But she had her false papers, right? She placed the child gingerly on the bed and peered through the window shade before cracking open the door.

"Can I help you?" she asked the officer as politely as she could muster.

"Outside," he said gruffly. "Bring your papers."

Olga's hands were shaking as she stepped back inside to grab her papers, the officer remaining in the doorway. She pulled the papers out from her valise and turned back around toward the door.

Just then, Evitchka awoke in a fit of coughing. Olga froze. She desperately wanted to go to her child, but knew she must follow the officer's command.

She could see the officer peek inside at the little blond-haired girl.

"Go take care of her," the officer said, and suddenly he was gone, on to the next room.

Olga shut the door, still shaking, and let out a deep, anguished sigh of relief. Her little Evitchka may have just unknowingly saved both of their lives.

Laci, unaware of his wife and daughter's close call, had made his way back into town. A coworker of his father-in-law's had agreed to help him hide. He just needed to find the man's apartment.

The town was swarming with police officers, and he tried his best to keep his head down and stay out of sight as he wound his way through the crowded streets. He had stopped for just a moment, wondering if he was heading in the right direction, when a police officer approached.

In Humenné, he knew all of the officers. Most were friends. Here in Nitra, he was a stranger.

"Papers!" the officer demanded.

He had his false papers in his coat pocket. He could have handed them over. But the papers connected him to Olga and Evitchka, who were still so close by. He made a split-second decision.

"I have no papers," he told the officer.

"Then drop your pants," the officer commanded.

This was it. Laci knew there would be no way out. The officer would see that he was circumcised, the clear and inescapable mark of a Jew. Filled with shame and foreboding, he did as the officer said and unzipped his pants, letting them drop to the ground.

"Your drawers too," the officer said impatiently.

Laci took a deep breath in, lowered his drawers and exposed himself to the officer and the surrounding onlookers.

"Let's go, Jew," the officer spat in his direction. "Pull up your pants."

The officer took him to the police station, tossing him into a cinderblock room already half full. Each day, more and more Jews were brought in until the room was nearly packed to the brim. He thanked God every day that none of them was Olga.

Still in the hotel room, Evitchka's cough had continued to worsen. There was no way for Olga to take the child to a doctor, but the loud whooping sound at the end of each coughing spell was unmistakable.

After three days of this, Olga could no longer stand it. She bundled up little Evitchka and headed into town to look for a drug store.

When she spotted the store on the corner, she hurried in and rushed to the back, scanning the shelves for anything that could help her daughter feel better.

"Did you hear the trains are finally running again?" she overheard the woman next to her say to her friend.

A flood of relief ran through her. She quickly gathered up the cough medicine and fever reducer and sprinted back to the hotel to pack her meager belongings. Nervous as she was, by that evening, Olga and Evitchka were on the train, heading west again for the nearly two-hour ride to Bratislava, capital of the Slovak Republic.

It was the middle of the night when mother and daughter pulled up in a taxi to the address that Laci had written for her on a slip of paper. Olga thanked the driver and waited for him to drive away before approaching the door of the cinder block house.

It had been years since she had seen her old friend Geza. They got on well in school, and she always found him charming, but, as a Catholic, he was no suitor for her — at least not one of which her parents would ever approve. She knocked, then waited. She knocked again. After about a minute, a light flickered on and shone through the small entryway windows.

Geza's wife opened the door. Klara Hajtas, a tall and handsome woman, took one look at Olga and the clearly sick child in her arms and quickly ushered them inside.

"Olga!" she said, embracing her. "What are you doing here so late? Where's Laci?"

Geza, having heard the commotion, had now appeared beside her, wearing a bathrobe and slippers.

"I don't know where he is," she said wearily. "We left him in Nitra to come here. He told us you could help us."

"Of course," Geza said, taking the child from her arms and wrapping her in a blanket. "We'll do everything we can."

6

September 1944

After about two weeks at the police station, Laci found himself in a terribly crowded cattle car. He wasn't sure where he was going, but for now it was nowhere because the train hadn't moved. After a sleepless night, he felt the rattle of the tracks beneath him, which was oddly comforting as he had already started to go stir crazy in the sealed container.

An hour later, he was ushered out of the car into the blinding sunlight. The signs around him told him he was at Sered. He knew he was still in the Slovak Republic — only about an hour from the capital and desperately close to Olga and Evitchka, yet so very far away from them — but the camp was clearly being run by SS guards, barking their orders in German.

He was put to work in a lumber yard, the irony of which was immediately apparent. He thought of his own lumber yard at home in Radvan, of the employees who so relied on him for their livelihood and who had always been loyal, right up until he was forced to abandon the business.

Out in this yard, with little supervision, there were ample opportunities to make a run for it. But it was risky. Better to keep his head down and hope that the Americans would come, he thought.

A month went by, and a visitor did come, but he wasn't an American. He recognized the man from his picture in the newspaper. It was Nazi Officer Adolf Eichmann.

He watched as Eichmann walked through the camp, and a short time later, many of the prisoners were loaded into another cattle car, but Laci was not among them. Instead, he was assigned to a new work detail.

In June, while they were still in Nitra, the Americans had bombed an oil refinery in Bratislava. At the time, Laci had seen this as a hopeful sign. The war must be ending soon, right?

Now, prisoners in the Sered camp were being relegated to clean up the mess. A nephew of Laci's, also in the camp, had submitted his name for the job. Though this work would bring him closer to his family, he didn't want to go — if the Americans did come and the war ended, wouldn't he be safer where he was?

So he said goodbye to his nephew and he stayed, continuing to work in the lumber yard as the number of prisoners around him dwindled, until the cattle car came for him, too.

This time, the dark compartment that he was ushered into was so full that he was unable to sit, only stand. The camp was nearly empty by that time, and he figured this transport would be one of the last.

He watched several people jump off the moving train, including a friend from back home. But Laci was afraid to jump, worried that he would never see Olga and Evitchka again if he didn't make it.

After two full days of standing almost statue-like, unable to move without bumping into the people around him, the train came to a halting stop and the doors of the cattle car opened.

"*Rausch, rausch, rausch,*" he heard the officers yell in German, swastikas clearly visible on their arms.

As he emerged from the cattle car tired, thirsty, and hungry, he saw raging fires and tall chimneys blowing dark smoke into the air. He had heard rumors of this place before, but he suddenly knew in his gut that everything he had heard was true. He had arrived at Auschwitz.

When he exited the cattle car, the sky dark, he was tossed immediately into a line divided into groups of three.

Laci found himself with two young brothers who looked to be about fourteen and seventeen. When they got to the front of the line, an SS officer gave them a quick once-over. "Left!" he barked to one brother. "Right!" to the other.

The younger brother, the meeker of the two, looked at the older with fear in his eyes. Without a moment's hesitation, the older brother jumped in. "No! Let me go with my brother."

"Fine, go," the officer said, obvious that he couldn't care less, and the boys walked off together.

You stupid boys, thought Laci. Then, he felt the officer's eyes turn in his direction, looking for any reason to toss him out like garbage.

In his thirties and no stranger to hard work, Laci was healthy and fit. But while in Nitra, he had a procedure to remove a fungus on his fingers. The time spent in the lumber yard at Sered had done him no favors, and his fingers still looked red and swollen. While in line, he had quickly removed the bandages. Now, he folded in his first three fingers ever so slightly as the officer looked him up and down.

He glanced at Laci, looked down at the list in front of him, and then yelled, "*Recht*!" Right.

He proceeded through the doors of a big hall not far from the gates. As he passed by a group of middle-aged women, their faces sunken in, he heard one whisper in his direction in Yiddish, "*Got helfn ir*" — God should help you.

Crammed into a crowded room, Laci was forced to take off his clothes. He did his best to avert his eyes from those around him, men and women of all ages with their dignity, far more than their clothes, being crudely stripped away.

Next, he was forced to line up, cold and naked, and wait for a shower. The icy water stung, but it mercifully washed off the dirt that had caked on his extremities. With that finished, the water still dripping from his body, he was directed into another line for rations and saw a man he recognized from Humenné who had disappeared nearly three years prior. The man gave him a nod of recognition and handed him a warm coat enveloping half a loaf of bread that looked and felt like a brick.

"Why are you giving this to me?" he asked the man quietly.

"Put it away, you will need it," he said.

Utterly fatigued and a bit delirious by this point, he saw still more friends from Humenné and nearly laughed out loud at their ragged appearance. "What are you looking at?" they asked him. "Soon, you'll look like this, too."

He was so tired that he barely registered what was happening when a series of letters and numbers were tattooed on his left forearm in black ink — B-12 934.

There was no sleep at all that first night. He wasn't even allowed to lie down, but he did everything he could to hide his exhaustion. Pushed outside early the next morning, the blinding sun stinging his eyes, Laci felt fortunate when he was chosen for a new work transport. One hundred and forty-five men were selected and, together, they walked several miles until they reached what appeared to be another camp, SS guards surrounding them with looks that dared them to slow down for even a minute.

At the camp, they found the remnants of what looked like a bombing. "Start cleaning!" one of the guards commanded. Laci looked mournfully at the heaping pile of debris in front of him.

Still, having been raised on long, hard hours in the lumber yard with his father, he picked up his shovel and got to work.

It took the men a few days to clear most of the rubble. Laci's back ached and his fingers had started to bleed, but he refused to utter a word about it. When the job was mostly finished, he heard one of the guards announce that the next day, they would only need forty-five men.

The next morning, the men lined up. He watched the guards striding back and forth, eyeing their selections. He spotted his wife's uncle, David, a few places down in line, trying to make himself shrink away from the guards' sights. David, he knew, had been the director of a bank back home. At the camp yesterday, he had watched as David's shovel had become emptier with each stroke, and then the guards beat him with it.

"David! Stand up tall. We need to go to work," he told him in a hoarse whisper.

"I won't make it another day out there," he groaned. "I can't do it."

Laci was among the group selected to finish the work. As they walked off, he looked back at David standing amongst the hundred or so men who remained. He sensed their relief at getting a pass from the backbreaking work.

When Laci's group returned to their barracks that evening, David and the other men they had left behind were nowhere to be found. They had been taken to the gas chambers to fulfill that day's quota, he later found out.

Laci had been at Auschwitz for about a week when another transport arrived. He watched from a distance early one morning as a stream of passengers straggled off the train, herded into lines heading toward the gates.

"Laci!" an old friend from the lumber business called out, hurrying in his direction. "Your parents, they're on the transport."

He felt the bile rise from his stomach to his throat, the sickness quickly turning to anger. His first thought was to run to them, to be comforted by their embrace, to say goodbye. For he knew right away that it would be goodbye — with his father's health and their advanced age, he was keenly aware that the Nazis would find no use for them in this camp.

Alas, he didn't. He couldn't. Though it pained him greatly, he stayed put. How it would break their hearts to know what had become of him. Let them imagine that he was still a free man, he thought. Later, his friend confirmed his fears — Moshe and Eugenia Ritter had been led straight to the gas chamber on the day they arrived, October 18, 1944.

7

October 1944

Olga and Evitchka had been in the care of the Hajtases for nearly a month, and they hadn't heard a word from Laci in all that time.

Geza, introducing them as his cousins, had been able to secure the mother and daughter an apartment on the second floor of one of the city's nicer buildings.

"Where's her husband?" the landlord had asked.

"Oh, he's fighting in the Slovak army," Geza assured him. As an employee of the railroad who was generally well-respected in the city, no one questioned his word.

Olga and Evitchka often joined Geza and Klara for meals, and one night, as they were sitting down to dinner, they heard a knock on the door.

Geza stood up to answer and, on his doorstep, found a woman wearing a black hat and coat with a Bible in her hand.

At first, Olga stayed out of sight, only picking up pieces of the hurried conversation between Geza and the woman as she peered carefully around the kitchen entryway. After a few minutes, however, she realized she recognized the voice and came bursting out excitedly into the hallway.

"Munci!" she exclaimed. "What are you doing here?"

Olga knocked off her sister-in-law's hat as she pulled her in for a tight hug, then excitedly stepped back to give her a once-over. Seeing anyone from home filled her with hope, and she thought maybe Munci knew of Laci's whereabouts. Munci seemed just as surprised to see her.

"I was staying with this nice family working as their housekeeper," she explained. "But the other day, a German soldier stopped by the house and came right up to me — got in real close — and said 'you look Jewish, are you Jewish?' I was so scared, I didn't know what to do. So I just mumbled that I didn't know what he was talking about. As soon as he left, I told the lady I had to leave."

Klara, having heard the commotion, was coming out into the hallway now to join them.

"The lady gave me this coat and hat, and a Bible and candle, and dropped me off at the train station," Munci continued. "It took eight hours to get here, and the Gestapo boarded the train at every station looking for papers from everybody. I was sitting there praying, trying to make myself look as quiet and pathetic as possible. They never said anything to me, and somehow I made it here. Laci and Olga always told me I could come to you for help. Please, will you help me?"

Geza and Klara exchanged a worried glance. They were already risking their lives having Olga and Evitchka there. Could they manage Munci, too?

"Olga, will you make Munci a cup of tea?" Klara asked her. "Give us a few minutes."

While Olga and Munci headed off to the kitchen — Munci telling her that, no, she hadn't heard from Laci — Geza and Klara went up the stairs to their bedroom.

"I'm not sure it's a good idea for her to stay," Geza said to his wife when they had shut the door. "We can't say she's our cousin, too."

"What if we say she's our maid?" Klara suggested. "Our maid did just leave, after all, and we could actually use her help."

"But what if someone starts asking questions?" Geza said hesitantly.

"Don't worry," Klara said. "She doesn't even look Jewish."

So Munci was allowed to stay, and she was indeed put to work. She cleaned, cooked, washed clothes in the basement, and brought the coal upstairs to the chimney. She accompanied Klara on her shopping trips, amused by the looks on the German soldiers' faces at the sight of such a beautiful woman as Klara. Munci would wear a kerchief on her head, doing her best to blend in as a lowly maid.

On one shopping trip a few weeks after her arrival, a soldier pulled Klara aside and started speaking with her in hushed tones. Munci was scared at first that he was asking about her, but then she noticed the way he leaned in toward Klara with a mischievous smile. Munci put her head down and quickly walked home.

She returned to find a message left with the neighbor that the Gendarmes had been there and would return the next day.

In a panic, Munci paced anxiously, waiting for Klara to return home to tell her the news. Geza was out of town on a business trip, she knew, and wouldn't be able to help.

The next day, as advertised, the officer returned. Klara, dressed in her finest attire, greeted him at the door. He brushed right past the "maid" as he stepped inside.

"We have it on good authority that there are Jews hiding here," the officer gruffly informed Klara.

"I don't know what you're talking about," she told the officer, shaken but firm.

"Where is Mrs. Olga Schneider?"

How did this officer know the name Olga had used on her false papers?

"There's no one here by that name," Klara said resolutely, a hint of flirtation in her voice. "Can I offer you a glass of wine?"

Half an hour later, the tipsy officer was back out the door with nothing to show for his visit. As soon as he left, Klara let out a deep, anguished breath.

"Please, we have to let Olga know they're looking for her!" Munci rushed to Klara and exclaimed.

"We can't, it's too risky," Klara said, visibly upset. "We should wait for Geza."

"Please, there isn't time. We must go now! Here, wait one second." Munci rushed out of the room and returned a moment later, her hand balled in a fist. She opened her palm to Klara and showed her a pair of diamond earrings.

"They're my mother's. Take them, save my sister-in-law and my niece," Munci begged.

Reluctantly, Klara called a cab, and she and Munci went to the apartment where Olga was staying.

"Olga, you must run!" Munci told her upon arrival. She recounted the story of the officer's visit.

Olga was aghast. The only person who knew her false name and hiding place outside of her family and the Hajtases was a close family friend and colleague of her father's in the vinegar business. Would he really have given her up?

She hadn't heard a word from her parents since they left Nitra, and she still hadn't heard from Laci. Her false papers were useless. She had nowhere to go.

"Please, what should we do?" Olga asked Klara desperately. Munci looked on tearfully, but couldn't offer any help herself.

"Geza will be back from his trip in a few days. He'll know what to do," Klara said, projecting as much confidence as she could muster.

"Until then," she said, the desperation evident in her voice, "you need to stay out of sight."

Olga was aghast. Where could she go? She thought of a friend she had met on her daily walks around the neighborhood. Perhaps she would help? With no time to gather more than a pack of diapers, Olga loaded Evitchka into her pram and left the apartment.

8

November 1944

Two weeks after arriving at Auschwitz, Laci again found himself packed inside a cattle car. There had been rumors circulating that the Russians were approaching Krakow, and the guards seemed determined to clear the barracks. He was chosen for the first transport.

The steady rattle of the tracks beneath him tore into his aching back, lying flat against the mucky cattle car floor. There was plenty of room to spread out, or there would have been if the four SS guards assigned to his car hadn't ordered their passengers to cram against the creaking walls, leaving the guards space to walk about and step on them at will.

After what felt like a long string of endless days and nights, the transport arrived in what he came to find was Oranienburg, just north of Berlin.

Laci's eyes barely had a moment to adjust to the bright sunlight before he was ushered into what looked like an airplane hanger, a sea of thousands of sullen faces filling the wide-open building. He clung to the familiar ones, the handful of people he knew from Humenné, and together they huddled in a corner, their body heat the best defense against their cold and damp surroundings.

The days wore on and the rations were meager, but there was no work to be done. Laci's strength recovered ever so slightly as he walked himself in circles around the hangar to keep his blood flowing. His resolve to return to Olga and Evitchka hardened by the day. Had they made it to the Hajtases, he wondered? Was his pretty Evitchka still safe in her mother's arms?

He could tell many of those around him were losing their grip on reality after a while, becoming stir crazy in the hangar-turned-prison. Laci knew how important it was to keep his wits about him.

The SS guards were constantly harassing the prisoners. Laci did what he could to keep his head down and mind his own business. Then one day, about two weeks into his time in the hangar, he happened to witness a man he recognized being hassled by two SS guards. He didn't know the man's name, but he knew that when they had been together at Auschwitz, this man had been what was known as a *machar* — a big deal. Clearly, here, he didn't curry the same favor.

The guards were yelling at the man, their questions flying out in an indecipherable German, but their tone unmistakable. The sheepish look on the man's face made it clear that he did, in fact, have something to hide, or maybe he just didn't care. Laci paused, standing about ten feet away, pretending not to watch as the scene unfolded, but unable to help himself.

Finally, it seemed, the guards tired of fighting with the man. They each grabbed him under one arm and dragged him toward the hangar's entrance, his feet skimming the floor as they went. He had been a larger man when Laci first encountered him, he remembered. Now, his clothes hung as loosely as his limbs as he was carried away without a fight.

Out of the corner of his eye, Laci thought he saw something shiny drop from the man's hand just as the guards picked him up. Leave it alone, he told himself, when at the same time he found his feet inching toward the spot where the man had once been.

Then, he was standing on the spot. Others milled about, unaware of this abrupt change in circumstance, but when Laci looked down, his heart started pounding. There on the dirt floor, already covered in dust, were four hefty diamonds.

Without thinking, Laci crouched down, quickly brushed the diamonds into his palm, and shoveled them into his pocket. He felt their physical weight almost immediately, used to carrying nothing on his person by this point. His fingers rolled back and forth over the four smooth stones as the weight of the dangerous secret he now carried hit him.

His mind raced. What luck to find something of such immense value here in this filthy hangar. How Olga would love these diamonds, how he would keep just one and sell three to give Evitchka a better life.

His brain clouded with hunger, he stood there in thought a full five minutes before the reality of his situation slowly dawned on him — diamonds, arguably the most valuable item in the world, had no real value here. He may never see Olga and Evitchka again. The only items of true value in the hangar were those you could eat.

Over the next few days, Laci ruminated over his dilemma, obsessively checking his pocket every few minutes, everywhere he went. Was there anything he could do to use these diamonds to his advantage?

He thought about barging into the kitchen and offering a trade. But he knew not everyone in there could be trusted, and if he traded with the wrong person, he would quickly become the guards' next victim.

Then, on the fourth day, Laci spotted a familiar face during his walk around the hangar. There was the man from Auschwitz, the *machar*, returned and looking no worse for the wear.

Laci suddenly knew what he had to do. He approached the man. Shaking inside, Laci leaned in close and projected as much confidence as he could muster as he whispered in the man's ear.

"I have something of yours," Laci hissed, reaching into his pocket, balling his hand into a fist and then opening it ever so slightly within the man's line of sight.

He saw a glimmer in the man's eye that matched the one on these precious stones.

"I'll give them back, but you'll look out for me, give me your soup when you can," Laci said, hoping the uncertainty he felt could not be heard in his voice.

The man nodded. Though Laci had no guarantees over the gentleman's agreement, in a place where every man was utterly self-interested, he also didn't have much to lose, so he handed over the diamonds.

Miraculously, the gamble paid off and the man did hold good to his word. Laci periodically found himself with extra servings of soup, just enough to sustain him through the month spent in the hangar.

Three days after the visit from the Gendarmes, Geza Hajtas returned home to find his wife in hysterics, his maid downtrodden and tearful, and his "cousin" and her daughter conspicuously absent.

"What happened here?" Geza demanded to know, hanging his hat on the coat rack.

Klara filled him in as the three of them sat around the kitchen table, his face aghast.

"Has the officer been back here?" Geza asked worriedly.

"Not yet," Klara said. "But who's to say he's not watching us from the street."

Geza sighed heavily. "Where are Olga and the child?"

"I don't know where they go during the day," Munci chimed in, "but at night they've been sleeping at a friend's apartment."

"Do you know the address?" Geza asked her.

Geza and Klara both understood the implications if they were to be caught helping Jews. Without question, they would be executed on the spot, or sent to the very camps that they were trying to help their friends avoid. Yet, the silent agreement between them held, their strong Roman Catholic faith drawing them together and guiding them on their mission. They would not be deterred.

After three days wandering the streets of Bratislava with little Evitchka in tow, Olga couldn't take much more. Her water canister had run dry and the chill in the air had soaked through their overcoats and left a near-constant shiver in its wake. She questioned her decision not to have left Evitchka at the farmhouse steps, to free her from this life of hiding.

Still, she had to stay close by, she knew, so that Geza could find her.

Alas, after a restless sleep on the hard mattress unceremoniously splayed out in her friend's living room, she heard a knock on the door and the whimper of a weakened Evitchka fighting herself awake.

Olga instinctively recoiled in fear as her eyes flew open. "Hide," her friend mouthed as she slowly walked toward the door, gesturing for Olga to move out of sight.

As quietly as she could, she inched toward the bedroom as her friend approached the door. Then she heard a familiar voice, and her whole body flooded with relief.

"Geza, I'm so, so sorry," Olga moaned as she ran out to greet him. "I thought we were being so careful. I could never have believed that my father's friends would give our names, your names. Will you ever be able to forgive me?"

"Olga, of course, please, are you okay? Evitchka?" he said, turning his attention to the toddler who gave him a light giggle.

"We're fine. Are you okay? Munci?" Olga asked hurriedly.

"Everyone's fine," he reassured her, "but we need to find you a new place to live."

Geza had secured new papers for Olga, and he brought her to the home of Mrs. Brown, a friend that he knew from his single days who lived on the outskirts of town. He had an inkling that this woman was just as inclined to help as he was, and he hoped that his instincts would prove correct.

As they stood together on the woman's front stoop, he knocked firmly.

"Dalka! So good to see you!" Geza exclaimed as his old friend answered the door. "I would like you to meet my cousin Olga and her daughter Evitchka."

"Nice to meet you," Dalka said, eyeing them suspiciously.

"I am hoping you can do us a favor," Geza began. "Olga's husband is off fighting in the army, and she needs a place to stay for a while. She's quite capable of helping around the house, and may be of good use to you here. Will you take her in?"

Dalka looked down at the cherub of a child, and back to the gentle face of her old friend. She hesitated for a minute before giving her answer.

"I can offer you a bed and little else," Mrs. Brown said. "But if you want it, it's yours."

9

December 1944

The stench in the hangar was becoming unbearable when, early one morning, the doors opened and a wave of cold, fresh air cascaded through. Dreary-eyed men rose from the dank floor, rubbing their eyes.

"Move out!" Laci heard the guards yelling in German. "Let's go, now, now!"

Laci locked eyes with his friends and silently started moving toward the exit. There had been five thousand people in the hangar upon arrival. He had no way of knowing how many fell to disease or starvation — or worse — over the last four weeks of their quarantine.

Laci followed the crowd of weary prisoners out into the yard, relishing the sight of the icy breath that escaped his own lips. The sun felt nearly blinding as he moved his hand to his forehead and squinted to survey the scene around him. As they stood there, waiting, his legs began to wobble slightly, but he ignored the urge to sit. Projecting strength was crucial, he had learned.

After what felt like hours, the guards ordered the prisoners to march out. Laci did as he was told, following in line.

They marched together for at least three miles, over the railroad tracks and through the city of Oranienburg until they reached a set of gates with signs that read "Sachsenhausen."

The camp reminded him immediately of his time in Auschwitz as he watched emaciated men and women wandering about with hopeless looks in their eyes. He expected to soon be among them, but instead of being stripped and showered and checked into the barracks as he had been at Auschwitz, Laci remained crammed into a building with his fellow prisoners from the hangar. There was no food and hardly any water. Were they waiting to be taken somewhere else? Or, more likely, were they waiting here to die?

The uncertainty lingered for two days before the guards broke them up into two groups. Those with last names beginning with "A" through "M" on one side, "N" through "Z" on the other.

Laci said a feeble goodbye to his friends from Humenné who were led away with the first group, and then he was alone, waiting. Another day passed before he was filtered onto a cattle car with the other "Rs" awaiting yet another unknown destination.

When he arrived at the new camp, no one from the first transport was there, and he could see that this camp was not yet fully built. He watched as lines of prisoners were sent out to work on the half-formed buildings.

There was nothing to eat, and after days of waiting and moving, they were starving. Finally, in the evening, the guards announced that they should pair up to share a ration. Laci sat down next to a young boy. The boy offered to procure the soup for the two of them, but after winding his way through the line, he never returned, and Laci just sat there, his stomach growling angrily.

He soon found that he was in Kaufering, in southern Germany west of Munich. There, evidently still viewed as among the strong, he was put to work again, forced to walk nearly four miles every morning to dig wide, deep holes, which he understood to be where the Nazis intended to build underground hangars for airplanes. It was backbreaking work, and each day Laci got weaker and weaker. Still, he refused to give up hope.

He ran into another man he recognized, named Manno, who had been the police chief back in Humenné. Here, it was evident that he was another *macher*. He ran roughshod over the uniform makers, the shoemakers; he even had a special kitchen where he could cook for himself. At Laci's worksite, there were charcoal-like bricks that Laci thought the police chief might find useful. He would steal them and bring them to the man in exchange for soup. One day, the guards spotted Laci and the policeman walking together. They nabbed Laci and beat him for seemingly no reason. The policeman was left unscathed.

After spending all day out at the worksite, Laci would return to camp and head to the kitchen to peel potatoes. For this, he received a little piece of bread and soup. He would be there until midnight most nights, even though his wakeup call was at 4:00 a.m., and he would pocket as many potato skins as he could and eat them later.

The guards were awful, but often the Jewish policemen — the Kapos — were even worse. One day, Laci was near the kitchen and grabbed two potatoes, and a Jewish policeman spotted him. He chased him into the kitchen, caught him, and beat him. There were girls in the kitchen who started to cry. The Germans already beat him, they wailed. You have to beat him, too?

One morning, Laci awoke to find what looked like three boils on his extremities. The next day, there were six. There was one barrack with doctors, and Laci reluctantly paid them a visit. There he found a Czech doctor, a Jew, who took one look at him and told him plainly, you will die.

He refused to accept this. With yet more boils raising their ugly heads, he went back the next day and found a doctor from Košice, another Jew, who, after assessing the situation, whispered to him in Slovak, "I will help you."

Laci lay down on the table, and the doctor gave him some kind of injection and drew blood. He asked him to return three days later, and when he did, the doctor injected him with his own blood that he had drawn. Soon, the boils disappeared.

He couldn't believe his luck and was hopeful that was the end of it. But, alas, the ordeal wasn't over. The injection site became infected, and Laci became so weak he could barely walk, let alone work. He went back to the Slovak doctor who said, "Okay, we have to open it."

The doctor took a plain knife, used a match to sterilize it, and sliced into the infected spot. What looked like a full glass of pus flowed from the wound before the doctor covered it in paper.

"You need to be very careful now," the doctor warned him. "You must let this heal, or else."

Laci didn't need to ask him what he meant by "or else." There were no antibiotics or any further treatments. If it didn't heal, he was done for.

Mercifully, the wound began to look and feel better each day. After a week, Laci had regained some of his strength.

After that, Laci tried his best to keep clean, fearing that any further health scare would lead to his end. He took showers as frequently as was allowed, and he would lie at night without bedding to avoid getting lice in his hair.

This was effective until a new transport arrived with another five thousand people who brought a renewed infestation of lice with them and, as a result of this, typhus quickly spread into the camp.

Laci had seen this before. At Auschwitz, and also in the hangar, he had seen fellow prisoners sickened by the horrible disease. First, he would notice their high fevers and angry red rashes, which made the illness nearly impossible to hide from the wandering eyes of the guards. If the disease itself didn't kill them, the Nazis surely would.

Suddenly, the prisoners were not allowed to work. They were stuck in quarantine, lying like fish in a row.

Every morning, the doctor would come and pick out the prisoners showing symptoms of typhus and take them away. One day, they would pick up from the right side of the room, the next day from the left. Laci played the odds and stuck to the middle.

Olga quickly found that she was not Mrs. Brown's only houseguest. There were, in fact, five other Jews hidden in the suburban apartment, though as far as Mrs. Brown knew, Olga was simply a friend who could be trusted with her secret.

Though Mrs. Brown was a generous host, there was little food to go around. Then one day, Geza came by with a letter addressed to her; it was from her father.

Olga hadn't seen or heard from her parents since they parted. As far as she knew, and hoped, they were still with their business associates in Nitra. Laci had taken care of the payments to cover their stay and ensure their safety. Olga had worried, of course, but assumed no news was good news. She opened the letter gingerly and saw her father's familiar scribbled handwriting.

"My Dearest Olga," the letter began. Already she could feel her eyes beginning to water.

Her parents had waited for months for the war to end, for the family to be reunited, her father wrote. Their hosts were kind, but the constant warnings blaring from the speakers in town had begun to wear on them: whoever is caught helping a Jew will have the same fate as a Jew. Finally, their fear overtook them, and their hosts told Morris and Anna it was time to leave.

Olga's tears drizzled on the paper as she read the next part. Her mother had gone out looking for a new hiding place and hadn't returned.

"No, no, no!" she cried to Geza, sobbing into his chest.

She couldn't bring herself to read on, so Geza picked up the letter and read the last few sentences before reporting back to her.

"Your father," he said gently. "He's going to give himself up to be with your mother. He wanted you to know."

"He can't! They'll kill them both!" Olga said hysterically. Olga wanted to run to him, to take the train to Nitra right then and demand that he change his mind. But deep down she knew that by the time she had received this letter, he would already be in captivity, or worse.

Geza urged her to take deep breaths.

"Your responsibility is to your Evitchka now," Geza said gently. "You need to take care of yourself so you can protect her. Just like your father is protecting you."

"What do you mean?" she asked, wiping her eyes.

He looked back down at the letter. "He says here that he's left some valuables in the vinegar factory in Nitra, hidden for you."

Olga took a moment to digest this news, but then realized, downtrodden, that they would be of no use to her anyway. She was barely safe here in Bratislava. She couldn't afford to take any risks right now.

"I'll get them for you, Olga," Geza told her determinedly.

"That's very kind," she told him, but you've already put your life and Klara's life in danger for mine. I'll not have you do anything more for us."

They said their goodbyes, Olga still clinging to the letter and resolving to put her focus into protecting her own daughter as her father would want. A couple of weeks later, Geza returned, this time with a bag in tow. He handed it to her.

Olga peaked inside and saw that the bag was filled with paper bills and gold pieces. A tidal wave of emotion washed over her — a longing for her parents, her home, the simple life they shared; gratitude for Geza and all that he was risking; determination to use these items to better her situation.

"But how did you ...?" Olga wondered incredulously.

"It was pretty simple, actually," he recounted. "I remember your father telling me once while we were still in school about the two men who had the best job in the whole company. They got to travel around to all the vinegar factories and fix things that weren't working. Well, I was able to get in touch with one of these men and accompany him on his visit to Nitra. I found these hidden right where Morris said they would be, and no one was the wiser."

Olga jumped up and gave Geza the strongest hug she could manage.

"You have no idea what this means to me, old friend. Thank you."

Olga knew that what her father had left and Geza had retrieved could mean the difference between starving and surviving for the seven Jews in Mrs. Brown's apartment. It also meant she had a bit of an insurance policy in case she found herself in trouble again.

With this, she felt emboldened to begin running errands on behalf of the group. She was a stranger in the city, after all. She had her new false papers, and she didn't look like a "typical" Jew. She would do the shopping every week, schlepping bags of food to the apartment, sweat dripping from her temples as she pushed Evitchka's carriage up the steep hill.

The chill of winter had settled over the city, but there was no fuel for heat with coal and wood so scarce. Each day, Olga took Evitchka out for a walk, carrying a basket between them. They broke pieces off of fences, gathered twigs and scraps of paper, anything that would burn. They savored every match they could find. When they came home, Olga made a little fire in her room and all the inhabitants gathered around it to warm their frigid hands.

Next, she used the fire to warm up water. She used the water to give Evitchka a bath, then she shared it amongst the residents: a young couple from Prague whose prior influence was evident in their stories from home but barely recognizable in their current state, a woman and her mother who huddled together for warmth each night, and an older lady who never complained and would bounce Evitchka on her lap while Olga tended to the fire.

All they could do was to keep on going, waiting and hoping that the tides of war would change and help would come.

10

January 1945

After a quiet Hanukkah celebration on their own at Mrs. Brown's apartment, the Hajtases invited Olga and Evitchka to join them for Christmas. Munci made carp, and they shut the blinds and huddled together near the warmth of the fire. Evitchka, nearly three now, bounced around from her aunt to her mother to her hosts.

"Settle down, my little Torpedo Head," Geza said playfully as he patted little Evitchka gently, and they all laughed.

It was a brief respite from the drudgery of daily life and worry, as Olga and Evitchka soon returned to their apartment in hiding, and Munci went back to her household duties.

One night not long after the new year, Munci was up late playing cards with Geza's brother when the doorbell rang. Two officers pushed their way inside and demanded that Munci leave with them.

"Please, Sir, I can show you my papers," Munci pleaded. But the men ignored her and hauled her off before Geza's brother even had a chance to react.

They took her to a house in a nearby town, dragging her inside and forcing her into a chair.

"Who are you?" the men demanded.

"I'm Maria Vallaly," Munci said resolutely, referencing the name on her false papers.

"You're Jewish," they declared.

"I'm not Jewish," Munci insisted, knowing they had no way to prove their assertion.

They opened her blouse. They didn't find anything, and she didn't know what they were looking for. Perhaps they thought she would be wearing a Star of David around her neck?

The men pulled her to a standing position and began hitting her on the backside, repeating their claims. Munci just stood there. She didn't cry or say a word.

"What are you?" they demanded to know, as they finally released her weakened body into the chair.

"I'm Greek Catholic," she told them confidently.

"Do you know all of the prayers?" they asked skeptically.

She recited them. She made the sign of the cross on her chest. She had been preparing for this for years.

She knew they didn't believe her when they started hitting her in the face. She could feel the blood oozing down her cheeks, and still she sat there. Growing frustrated, the men picked her up from the chair and threw her down a set of stairs, locking the door behind them.

In the freezing cold basement, she quickly found she wasn't alone. A doctor from Košice was there, and he did his best to clean her wounds. Each time he dabbed at her face with a wet towel, she recoiled from the sting.

The next day, the officers brought her upstairs again for another round of beating. Each time they called her a Jew, she denied it. She had seen enough already in her twenty-six years for a lifetime. She could be strong.

That night, when they shoved her back into the basement, the doctor was gone, and the silence was deafening.

This went on for another three days with no food and just a little water to sustain her. By the end, she knew they still had no proof of her apparent guilt. On the fourth day, expecting another beating, she instead received a proposition.

She could hear them whispering over her shoulder in German before they spoke, not realizing she understood. "Look at her hands, they're cold and broken," they said. "She doesn't look Jewish."

"We need girls to clean and work around the house," one of the men said.

"I'll do it," she interrupted. Survival was the only thing on her mind at this point. Her parents, Laci, Olga, and Evitchka. She had to make it back to help them.

She quickly came to realize this house was once occupied by Jews before it was overtaken by the Gestapo. And it had become somewhat of a way station before Jews were taken on, to Auschwitz she presumed.

Munci worked and cleaned harder than she had ever worked in her life. She scrubbed the brown leather coats of the Gestapo officers with shoe polish. She climbed onto the eaves in the freezing cold to clean the third and fourth-floor windows. She cleared hundreds of empty wine bottles abandoned by the officers.

There was little to eat — mostly horse salami and frankfurters. Black coffee in the morning and a piece of bread. A Catholic woman with a Jewish husband who was working in the kitchen took a liking to Munci and would give her extra food. She would squirrel it away and sneak it up to the other Jews if she heard someone was sick.

Thirty to fifty Jews would be brought to the house at a time. If they spoke freshly to the officers, they would be beaten, or worse. Munci washed the blood out of the carpets. "If you tell anyone, we'll kill you," the officers told her repeatedly.

She never saw anyone being killed, but would hear the screaming coming from the office and the eerie silence that followed.

In the spring of 1945, the Soviets invaded Bratislava. The Czechoslovakian government, which had been forced out when the Slovak Republic was established, had been operating for years in exile to try to return the country to its pre-war boundaries. One year prior, the Czechoslovak leader, Edvard Beneš, had signed an agreement with the Soviets stipulating that Czechoslovak territory liberated by Soviet armies would be placed under Czechoslovak civilian control.

An attempt to resist German troops had been tried, and failed, in central Slovakia in late 1944. Partisan resistance forces, with the help of the Soviets and Allied powers, battled over the course of six weeks against German occupation. The German forces proved too strong and better organized.

After the fighting ceased and the Germans regained control, many partisans and their families were hanged for their participation. Villages suspected of collaboration with the insurgent army were burned down.

This led Olga and her housemates to view this new turn of events with trepidation. They lay low as fighting ensued, waiting to see who would come out with the advantage.

The couple from Prague was insistent that their saviors would soon arrive. Olga was not convinced, and the longer the bombs fell, the less interested she became in fleeing to the shelter when they did. It was futile, she thought. *Que sera, sera.*

She resumed her walks with Evitchka, brazenly moving about the neighborhood simply for the chance of human interaction. She had become depressed and bitter, and therefore a little daring. Still, she often found herself practicing the Hail Mary Catholic prayer over and over with Evitchka as she walked, making sure they both would be ready to recite it confidently to any officer who tried to stop them.

One day, she came across a Communist Party member she knew from Humenné.

"Mrs. Ritter, why do you walk the streets?" the party member asked her quietly. "Not everybody is as good as I am. You should not be seen out here."

On another occasion, she saw a friend being led away by the Gestapo. Their eyes met, but then the woman looked away, refusing to acknowledge they knew each other so they wouldn't take Olga, too.

When the Gestapo came to the house one day — not the Germans, but their Slovak counterparts, members of the Slovak Expeditionary Army Group — Mrs. Brown asked her to translate since she didn't speak Slovak. Instead of being fearful, Olga saw it as a challenge. After all this time, Mrs. Brown still didn't know that she was Jewish.

At the end of her third month working for the Gestapo, Munci caught wind that the Germans were running from Budapest. The Soviets were pushing them hard.

A few days later, she and her fellow housemates finished their work for the day and went down to the cellar to rest. They did notice the lack of German music playing upstairs, but they didn't pay much attention.

Later that night, they were awoken by the creaking of the stairs and were surprised to see a German soldier making his way down. They quickly huddled together in fear, but were surprised when the soldier spoke to them in Czech. "Why are you sitting here?" he asked. "No one is watching you."

Astounded for a moment, they quickly came to their senses, slipped into their shoes, and ran up the stairs and out the door. The sound of shots being fired and bombs dropping seemed to be coming from all directions. The three men immediately took off, and Munci was left there with another woman wondering what to do.

She thought for a moment, and then made a decision in her own mind. They would go to the Hajtases.

It took about a day to make their way back to the house, taking back roads and detours to avoid the line of fire, and when they arrived, they found Geza and Klara packing their bags. Her former hosts were overjoyed to see her, and quickly told her the plan. They were heading to a suburb of Bratislava to wait out the battle that was overtaking their city.

Bombs still flying around them, they drove to a villa owned by a friend of Geza's.

The woman quickly ushered them inside, and they headed straight down to the basement. There, Munci was shocked to see familiar faces — Olga and Evitchka were in the basement, too.

The sisters-in-law stared at each other, almost in disbelief to see the other in one piece. Then they both ran in and embraced, tears streaming down their faces. Munci picked up the giddy child and held her close, kissing her cheeks, her forehead, and her little hands.

For two days, they huddled together in the cramped basement. The space was so tight, they all had to lie on their sides to make room for the others to sleep.

After two days, the explosive sounds subsided, and they cautiously made their way upstairs to wait for news. It wasn't long before Mrs. Brown received word about what had taken place. The Soviets had captured the airport, and the government of the Slovak Republic had fled the capital. The Germans had tried to fight back, destroying all the major bridges crossing the Danube River, but it wasn't enough. The Soviets had driven the German troops out and were now in control of Bratislava.

11

April 1945

By spring, there was a rumor going around that Oranienburg was about to be evacuated. Laci had done what he could to keep his strength while trapped inside, but deep down he knew he was fighting a losing battle. Worse yet, his shoes were nearly worn through.

He went in search of the Jewish police chief from Humenné, Manno. He was from a good family. His brother had been Laci's schoolmate. He had to help him, right?

Laci first checked Manno's private room. His mouth nearly watered at the sight of the boots and shoes stacked against the wall. A beautiful girl from Budapest, a doctor's daughter and Manno's girlfriend, was there lying in bed. But no Manno.

Finally, Laci tracked him down.

"Manno, listen, we are evacuating. Maybe we're going to hell, I don't know, but if there's any chance that we will live, please give me a pair of shoes," Laci begged. "I'll give you so much gold when we get home."

Manno looked at him for a moment, appearing to consider the offer, and then shrugged it off. "Sorry, I can't help you," he said gruffly.

Sure enough, only days later, the remaining prisoners were ordered to their feet. Laci quickly shot up and awaited instructions, expecting to be sent straight to a cattle car. He walked out into the sunlight, squinting his eyes, but there was no train in sight.

"March!" the guards ordered. "Move out!"

He looked down at his boots, his left big toe poking out, already feeling the scrapes of the rocks beneath his feet, and was gripped with fear. They were walking.

He, of course, had no idea where he was heading. After the first day, he nearly collapsed on the ground, his feet throbbing, huddling with his fellow prisoners for warmth against the chill of the early spring air as they spent the night outside.

Late the next evening, they arrived at Dachau, another concentration camp in Germany, but there was no room for them, and the guards ordered them to trudge on.

After another frigid night outside and more hours spent walking on wobbly legs, they came to another camp. The signs announced they had arrived at Munich-Allach.

The SS guards rushed them inside and then left them. The new arrivals were greeted by the camp's current prisoners. "Where are you from?" they asked hopefully, undoubtedly searching for any news from home.

Laci collapsed into a chair.

"Why don't you lie down?" one of the other prisoners advised him. "You look very weak."

"I'm afraid to lie down," Laci told him. "I don't want to get lice."

The man insisted, and Laci felt his resistance lifting.

So Laci lay down. By the next morning, he felt the tiny bugs crawling through his hair and on his clothes, and the SS men had disappeared.

They were awakened by shouting, "The Americans are here, everybody run!"

A shot of adrenaline spread through Laci's body. He tried to stand, but then he realized he couldn't. He tried again and made it to his feet, but he was unable to force his legs forward.

As the room began to clear, he spotted an American soldier coming in his direction. Was it a mirage? Had his months of suffering and scraping by finally come to an end?

Alas, there was the soldier, now right in front of him, and Laci reached up gratefully to accept the piece of chewing gum and pack of cigarettes that he offered. He practically tore open the piece of gum, its sweet, minty flavor giving his insides a jolt and moistening his dry, cracked throat.

The next few days were a blur as the Americans cleared the camp and brought the prisoners to another facility where they were given all the food they had been craving. It was too much food, and it wreaked havoc on many of their wrecked bodies. Laci watched his diet carefully.

A week or so later, two American officers came through and began registering the French and Czechoslovaks for transport out. Laci could still barely walk, but he could feel the hope rising in his chest. He was going to see his family again.

Until, upon examination from an American doctor, he heard the news that he had been dreading for months — he had typhus.

At first, the fact that the Soviets had succeeded in overtaking Bratislava seemed like good news. The feeling of relief was short-lived, however, as Olga and her housemates quickly became aware of the new danger they were facing.

The first Soviet officer who came to their apartment took the watch right off the wrist of the man from Prague. The women hid in the basement in fear that they would be raped. There were rumors that the Soviets could drink the Germans under the table, and remnants of their rowdy parties littered the city.

Meanwhile, fighting continued in the German-occupied parts of the country and in the Tatra Mountains, which created a blockade preventing Olga and Munci from traveling back east. Finally, a month after the Soviets gained control of Bratislava, the border village of Makov was the last to be liberated in the former Slovak Republic. The Czech government was back in control, and it was time for Olga, Munci, and Evitchka to figure out their next move.

It was then, as their fear mercifully subsided, that the worry began to set in. What had happened to the rest of their family? Would they have a home to return to?

Munci still didn't know what had become of her parents. For months, she had assured herself they must be safe; Laci had paid for their safekeeping at the home for the elderly.

She hadn't heard anything from her brother Jack either, and she knew Olga was sickened to think of her own parents' fate. And where in the world was Laci?

"I can't send you home," the American doctor told Laci.

Tears formed in his eyes, but with little fight left to protest, he nodded resolutely. The next day, a pair of American soldiers picked him up from his cot and loaded him into the trunk of a Jeep en route to a field hospital. Before he left, he caught the ear of a man he had worked with in the camps who was heading to Bratislava on the first transport.

"Please, let my wife know I'm alive," he implored.

Laci knew it was a longshot, but the man agreed he would, and he waved at Laci as the Jeep pulled away.

As terrible as he felt, the field hospital was the most wonderful place he had ever seen. With a bed and clean white sheets, it might as well have been a luxury hotel. Or maybe heaven, he wasn't quite sure.

For hours, he slipped in and out of sleep. When he opened his eyes, two doctors were standing at his bedside.

"Look at his skin, it's like paper," the American doctor mused, pinching his forearm.

"He's thin as a rail," he heard another doctor mumble.

Laci watched as they hung a fresh bag from his IV poll and walked away, their heads shaking.

Laci's brother Jack had also spent the intervening months desperately hoping to reunite with his family. Like his brother, he knew his wife and daughter would be safer without him, and so insisted that they stay apart. Unlike his brother, Jack had somehow managed to evade capture, constantly on the move, hiding as best as he could on farms and in the forest.

Roszi, tasked with protecting their child, was very resourceful and used her false papers to convince families to take in a lonely Catholic woman and her young daughter. When soldiers would come by, instead of giving them trouble, they would often ask to play with little Judy – with her blue eyes and blond hair, she reminded them of their own children they left behind.

Remaining to the east of the Tatras, Jack, Roszi, and Judy were the first to reunite and begin to rebuild their life in Humenné when the war ended. A few weeks later, they were overjoyed when Munci, Olga, and Evitchka, finally able to make the long journey, arrived home.

With the whereabouts of Laci still unknown, Jack turned to the Joint Distribution Committee, an organization formed to help Jewish refugees, for assistance.

He traveled to Bratislava, and he was sitting in the waiting room at the Joint one day when a man approached the counter and started talking about a friend from Humenné who wanted his wife to know his whereabouts.

"Well what's the man's name?" he heard the woman at the desk ask him.

"Leopold Ritter," he answered. Jack practically fell off his chair.

He rushed to the counter. "Leopold Ritter, you say? That's my brother!"

Jack pressed the man for details, thanked him profusely, and all but ran to the station to catch the very next train home. Olga nearly doubled over in relief when she heard the news.

"He's okay!" she shouted, hugging Jack and then grabbing Evitchka and swinging her around.

"Olga, there's more," Jack cautioned, and Olga's face fell. "Laci's very sick."

12

May 1945

While she waited anxiously for further word, Olga slowly began picking up the pieces of her house, which had been ransacked by the Nazis but was mercifully still standing. The house was eerily quiet, the vinegar factory in shambles. With no further word from Laci and no indication of what had become of her parents, she did her best to make it feel like a home for Evitchka.

Slowly, Jews in town had begun to return from the death camps. Each day, Olga and Evitchka would go down to the train station, scanning the crowds for any sign of familiar faces.

Every day for four weeks, they returned home disappointed. They had watched a few families reunite as a bedraggled man or woman would step onto the platform. But most of the onlookers would turn back toward town with sunken looks in their eyes. There were precious few children in the crowd.

Then, one overcast afternoon, a stooped old woman stepped off the train. At first, Olga didn't recognize her, but the thin, gray-haired woman was coming in her direction.

As she came closer, Olga's eyes widened. "Anu?" she asked nervously.

"Olga, my daughter," she said, embracing her.

Tears of joy flowed down both women's faces. Neither had known the fate of the other, thinking they would never see each other again.

Then Anna turned her attention to her granddaughter. A toddler when she had last seen her, Evitchka was now a sturdy three-and-a-half-year-old.

"Babi has something for you," she said to the child, opening her tattered cardboard suitcase and pulling out something wrapped in newspaper.

When Evitchka unwrapped the package, her eyes glowed. It was a doll exquisitely dressed in a traditional Slovak peasant costume with a full, twirling blue skirt and a flowered blouse with pleated sleeves.

Olga wondered what her mother had done to procure this doll. But she was heartened, nevertheless, by the delighted look on Evitchka's face.

Olga was truly shocked to see her mother — or the shell of her mother that appeared before her — and gingerly led her home.

At first, Anna refused to talk about what had happened to her since her capture; but over the next few weeks, she reluctantly began to share the broadest strokes of her account, purposefully leaving out details she knew would be too painful for her to speak or Olga to hear. Those she would always keep to herself, she vowed.

Anna and Morris were reunited at the detention center, as he had hoped, but then loaded onto different cattle cars and separated from that point on. Upon arriving at Auschwitz, he was nowhere to be found, and it was days before she discovered his fate — he had been trampled to death in the cattle car.

This was the first confirmation Olga had of her father's death. Tears streamed down her cheeks as she listened to the rest of Anna's story.

Anna, devastated by the loss of her husband, was sent to work in a munitions factory at the camp along with her sister Ilka, who had been rounded up at about the same time.

For seven days a week, from daybreak to nightfall, Anna worked on the factory assembly line. She was given little to eat – mostly thin broth and potatoes – but she and her sister were resourceful. They found some old *shmattas* — head coverings — to wear, and were able to take out the lining to sell for a potato. They took the potato and mixed it with margarine and put it on the hard bread to make it more edible. They slept on a rough wooden platform with four or five other prisoners.

Then, in early spring, Anna became very ill with typhus, which she thought surely would be the end of her as she had seen the sick women around her sent straight to the gas chamber. But timing was on her side; only days later, the camp was liberated and Anna, feverish and nearing delirium, was swept into the arms of an American soldier and taken to a U.S. field hospital where she was treated and ultimately recovered.

Olga could feel her mother's anguish as she recounted the events of the last several months.

"How lucky I am that you're here with me now," Olga told her, her voice full of love and amazement at her mother's strength.

A tired look spread across Anna's face, and she once again became silent. Olga leaned in to give her a tight hug and then left her to her thoughts.

Laci had fallen into a deep sleep and, miraculously, the next time he opened his eyes, he could feel some of his strength returning. Against all odds, he continued to improve, and a few days later, he asked his doctors for a cigarette and they laughed.

After ten days, he had made remarkable progress, and the doctors said they couldn't keep him any longer — they needed the bed. They sent him off to another facility to recuperate.

As his body healed, his mind also began to refocus. He wept for his parents, a shock he had not had one moment to process. He wondered about his siblings. And, most pressing, he ached for Olga and little Evitchka. Had Geza been able to protect them? Did they know what had become of him?

The better Laci started to feel, the hungrier he became. In fact, he was ravenous. But he did his best to heed the warning from a Romanian doctor he came across: Don't eat so much, your heart can't take it.

Instead, after he was sent back to his barracks a few days later, he kept busy as everyone's translator.

The Americans were registering the former prisoners for transport again, and they were specifically looking for Czechoslovaks. Anxious to be released, everyone around him — Hungarians, Romanians and the like — were claiming to fit the bill. When it came time to speak to the officers in the proper language, they turned to Laci to be their voice, and he was happy to oblige.

Then, alas, it was his turn. He was finally going home.

13

June 1945

The Americans came and picked up the remaining prisoners from Laci's barracks, transporting them in trucks to Czechoslovakia. They spent the night in Pilsen before arriving in Prague the next day.

For Laci, this was the end of the line for the transport, as far as he was concerned. He emerged onto the city streets, breathing the familiar air in deeply. He was a long way from Humenné still, yet he felt at home.

He made his way to the train station, savoring his first taste of freedom in more than eight months, walking at his own pace and meandering a little. He jingled the few coins in his pocket, given to him by the Americans, which should be just enough to get on the train.

He arrived to find the trains weren't running on schedule, so he spent the night on the floor of the station. By the time he boarded a train the next morning, his stomach was audibly rumbling.

A man sat down next to him, whom he soon learned was a Christian from Radvan who had been taken to Germany. They got to talking, and soon the man was sharing his bread, butter, and sugar.

It was enough to hold Laci over, and in each major city where the train stopped, the Joint Distribution Committee was there, offering meals to the Jewish passengers. At the first stop, Laci brought his new Christian friend in line with him. Please, he has been so helpful to me, give him lunch, Laci implored. And they did.

The next day, the train arrived in Bratislava. Before he could disembark, a Jewish lady on the train saw how thin he was and offered him some money. Never one to take charity, he knew this time he needed to accept her offer. Thanking her profusely, he left the train and began to look for a hotel to spend the night. He couldn't wait to see Olga and Evitchka, hoping to find them with the Hajtases, but he knew he needed to get himself together first.

Each hotel he arrived at, however, was full of Soviet officers, leaving no vacancy. Finally, too tired to trudge on, he gave up and slept a few hours in a plastic chair in a hotel lobby.

As more survivors arrived home with stories to tell, Olga came to find out that Laci had been in Dachau in the hospital recovering. She wanted desperately to go see him, but Munci put a stop to it.

"No, you have a child, a family, I have nobody," Munci told her resolutely. "I don't care what happens to me. I will go."

The next day, she packed her bags and took the train back to Bratislava. After a few days of traveling, she made it to Geza and Klara's house, where she planned to stay until she got papers to go to Germany.

The papers finally came through, and the morning she was supposed to leave, somebody rang the doorbell.

At first, she was scared, ready to hide under the bed in case it was a Soviet soldier. But Geza was out and Klara was in the shower. She collected herself and prepared for trouble. The bell rang again.

When she opened the door, she saw a man standing there, small, skinny, barely recognizable. Still, she would know that face anywhere.

Munci started to scream. Klara came running out of the bathroom, alarmed, just in time to witness Munci pulling a gaunt man in the doorway into a tight embrace.

"Laci, is it really you?" she screamed, hugging him once again.

"Olga? Evitchka?" he asked hurriedly.

"They're okay. They're back in Humenné waiting for you," Munci told him. "The Hajtases, they saved them. They saved us all."

Munci took Laci to a restaurant while Klara got dressed, and they waited for Geza's return. She didn't think he would ever stop eating. He was just so hungry. He weighed in at only seventy-eight pounds, he told her.

When they got back to the house, Geza and Klara were waiting.

"My friends, how can I ever thank you for what you have done for our family?" Laci said, reaching out his hand to firmly shake Geza's before pulling him into a warm hug. "I will do whatever I can to repay you. You are part of our family forever."

The next morning, after a good night's sleep, Munci and Laci began the journey home. When they arrived at the train station in Humenné, Laci looked around anxiously. His wife and daughter would be there, he knew it.

Finally, he saw them. Olga was holding Evitchka in her arms, and they were waving excitedly from the platform.

Laci darted through the crowd until there they were, standing in front of him.

Words were for later. He leaned in to kiss Olga tenderly, and Evitchka, whom she had placed on the ground, now clung to his leg.

"Apu, I missed you," the girl proclaimed and Laci, with what was left of his strength, picked her up into his arms and carried her home. As they walked, he listened to his little girl, a toddler when he had left her, talking a mile a minute. Oh, how much he had missed. But how very fortunate he was to be here now.

In the weeks that followed, the number of people returning from the camps dwindled until the trains were once again empty. Desperate family members still waited on the platforms regardless. But it soon became clear that no one else was coming.

Before the war, there were about two hundred Jewish children in Humenné. Now, it seemed, including little Evitchka, there were six.

14

August 1945

The screams kept her awake at night, and Munci couldn't take it anymore.

With her own house destroyed, Munci had gone to live with Laci and Olga in their house in Humenné. Olga's mother Anna and her aunts — Ilka, who had been with Anna in Auschwitz, and Roshi, who had gone into hiding — were living there, too.

Munci was assigned a room with Ilka, who had lost her son and husband in Auschwitz. At night, Munci would bury her head in the pillow as Ilka's anguished yells rang out in her sleep.

"Please," Munci said to her brother. "I have to go somewhere, I can't stay here."

Though Laci was reluctant to see her off, he called a friend who lived in Prague, a lawyer, who agreed he could use Munci's help babysitting. So Munci said her tearful goodbyes to her brother, sister-in-law, and young niece and headed off to the city. She cooked for the lawyer's family and tended to the child, all the while plotting her next move.

The day the American consulate opened in Prague, Munci was in line to register for a visa. By the time she reached the front of the queue, she was already number four hundred. A cousin in America who was big in the necktie business agreed to sponsor her, and so she waited.

In the summer of 1946, Munci's visa came through. Laci gave her money to get to Sweden, where she boarded a boat in the third-class cabin. The smell was nearly unbearable, and she was sick for the entire voyage, but after nine days she caught a glimpse of the Statue of Liberty and thought, "Thank God, I'm here."

While Munci settled into her new life, Laci and Olga were still trying to reclaim theirs.

Upon returning to the house, they dug around in the yard and were surprised to find their prized possessions still intact. The silver candelabra was once again lit on Friday nights, though they missed Morris terribly each time they said the prayers.

Laci and Jack took the train to Radvan and found their lumber yard in serviceable condition. They hired hands and got to work reopening the business.

In addition, Laci was now responsible for the vinegar factory. The factory was destroyed during the war and parts to fix it up were scarce, but the directive from headquarters was that the factory owners should help each other rebuild. For two years, Laci traveled across the country to different factories, asking each one what they could spare. By 1947, the factory was up and running, and it looked like Laci and Olga would settle comfortably.

After the war, Czechoslovakia had been reestablished and the Communist Party had formed a coalition government and taken key positions. For the most part, they didn't pay the Jews any mind. Then one day, word spread that a Jewish man in Humenné was causing trouble, and the government wanted him hanged. They wanted a

Jewish witness to speak out against the man, and Laci was surprised when they approached him.

Then he learned why they were asking. The man in trouble was Manno, who had refused him boots at the camp in Germany.

While he was mulling it over, sitting on a park bench and gathering his thoughts, someone sat down next to him. It was Manno.

"Please, Ritter, I don't want to die," Manno begged.

"You wouldn't help me when I needed it, why should I help you now?" Laci asked him.

"You know what it was like in there. I did what I had to do to survive," Manno said by way of explanation.

It wasn't exactly the apology he was looking for, but Laci sighed. "Disappear," he told him. "Leave Humenné and stay away."

"I will," the man promised. He was good to his word.

So Laci went back to work and, while riding the train to Radvan one day, he spotted a face he recognized from the newspapers. It was a man by the name of Dvořák, son of the famous composer. He knew this man was a big shot, having bought a lot of forest land from the Czechs.

They started talking, and Laci told him he was in the lumber business. They got so friendly that Dvořák invited him on trips and helped him skirt around the limits of how many fields could be culled in a year. He, in turn, supplied Dvořák and his friends with hard-to-find salami on their hunting excursions.

The lumber yard and vinegar factory were both turning a profit by this time, and Laci truly felt like things were looking up. He was doing so well that when the Hagannah — the main Zionist paramilitary organization in Mandatory Palestine formed to defend Jewish settlements — asked for money, he became one of the organization's largest contributors.

HIAS, the Hebrew Immigrant Aid Society, caught wind of this and solicited him as well, and he gave to them, too.

Overall, he was happy with life in Czechoslovakia. Evitchka had just turned six and started kindergarten. Then in February 1948, the country was overtaken by the Communists.

After the war, the newly reestablished country had looked favorably on the Soviets who had liberated them. Eduard Beneš, who became president when the war ended, had signed a friendship treaty with the Soviets in 1943 while working with the government-in-exile. While the Communists were not in power, they held a number of high-ranking government positions. In the 1946 elections, the party showed its popularity by bringing in thirty-eight percent of the vote.

Then, in the summer of 1947, Czechoslovakia began to seek out aid that the United States was offering to help European countries rebuild after the war. This upset the Soviets, who said that by accepting the aid, Czechoslovakia would be in violation of the friendship treaty. This, compounded with economic problems, objections by farmers to collectivization, and scrutiny of the fast pace of industrialization led the Communist party to fall out of favor. By January of 1948, support among the people had dropped to twenty-five percent.

The Communists within Czechoslovakia would not be deterred. They began trying to convince citizens that the Slovak Democratic Party was connected directly to the Nazis. They claimed that during the Nazi era, supporters of an independent state of Slovakia had conspired against the nation. The police, overrun by Communists, cited treason and arrested three hundred and eighty citizens, mostly from the Democratic Party. Arrests continued of other high-ranking Democrats for no apparent reason. They used their leadership positions in departments like the Ministry of the Interior to appoint more Communists inside the government. The Democratic ministers tried to fight back, but their Communist counterparts refused to give in.

With trade unions behind them, the Communists set up armed

"action committees" in industrial plants, farms, and villages. On February 20, 1948, a people's militia with seven thousand members was formed. The twelve non-Communist ministers in the government resigned, believing that they would be able to form a new government.

Instead, violence erupted in the streets. The trade unions rioted in Prague, attacking Democratic offices. The army, which could have quelled these demonstrations, was run by a Communist general to whom the Soviets pledged their support. Soon, the Red Army had taken up positions on the Czechoslovak border.

Afraid that the Soviets would intervene or that a full civil war would break out, President Beneš stood back. He also feared renewed power from Germany if the Soviets did not maintain control in the region. The Soviet style of Communism would be moderate, he thought. Under threat of a general strike and punishment for dissidents, Beneš reluctantly accepted the Communist Party's set of proposals and allowed the party to take control.

From that point on, no opposition to the Communist Party was allowed. Citizens who tried to fight back against the new laws were fired or arrested.

The Ritters had eyed the problems in the government with trepidation, but they began to slightly relax as months passed after the winter-time coup and nobody bothered them. That is until July of 1948, when two men in formal dress knocked on the door of the vinegar factory.

"We are from the government. We are nationalizing this factory," one of the men said.

"The house, too," the other man said gruffly. "For the office."

From Laci's dealings up until this point with the Communists, he understood this to mean that his private property that he had worked and paid for was being "returned" to the nation without any retribution or compensation.

"But we've heard about you. You're a decent man," the first official said. "We could allow you to stay on here as manager."

"Thank you," Laci said carefully. "I'll consider it."

He knew, however, that he wasn't going to consider it. After all that his family had been through, this was the last straw. They needed to get out of there, and quickly.

But where would they go? Other cities in Czechoslovakia would have the same problems. He could go elsewhere in Europe, he supposed, but he was not so trusting after all that had happened during the war. Then he remembered — shortly after liberation, he had registered for an American visa, just in case.

The next day, he went to the American consulate in Prague. Even with many of his siblings and cousins there, he never saw himself living in America. The visas, he knew, were distributed on a numbers system based on the time of registration. He gave his number. "How long will the wait be for a visa?" he asked.

The worker at the consulate was surprised. "That's a very low number," she told him. "You could have been in America a long time ago."

"Well, how long will it take now?" he asked again.

"Four to six months, probably more like four," the worker said. "But you'll need your passports."

15

January 1948

Jack and his family had left for America just before the Communist takeover. Unlike Laci, Jack knew he wanted to be in the States. When he married Roszi in 1941, they had applied for visas, but with the war already ongoing and the list long, the approval never went through.

With the lumber business in good hands, by early 1948 Jack was once again ready. The cousin in the tie business who had vouched for Munci also vouched for him, and he was surprised when the visas came through quickly. Then he realized many of the people who had applied before the war were now gone.

He got the visas, but the country was price gouging on passports at the time, particularly for Jews. Still, he would do anything he could to get out, and he handed over the five thousand crowns that were demanded.

The family of three said their goodbyes — Judy hugging her cousin and closest playmate Evitchka tightly — and made their way to Germany, where they were supposed to board the Queen Elizabeth I for the transatlantic trip. When they arrived, however, they were told something had broken on the ship, and it would be at least two weeks until it was repaired.

"I'm out of here," Jack said. "Put me on any ship you've got."

The only boat leaving over the next couple of days was an old warship called the Ernie Pyle. Women were relegated to one side of the ship, men to the other, and they slept in triple bunks. Six-year-old Judy spent the entire thirteen days throwing up, and by the time she reached Ellis Island, she was feverish. The doctors nearly didn't let her in, but her parents, mercifully, convinced them.

Laci knew what Jack had spent on his passports two months prior, and so he was prepared for a hefty sum when he arrived in Bratislava in January of 1949. But he was aghast when he heard that the cost had gone up even further — to fifty thousand crowns. And that wasn't all.

"Have you paid your taxes?" they asked him.

"Yes, of course," Laci said.

"Have you paid your taxes for this year?" they asked again.

"I'm leaving, I won't even be here," he told them.

"You don't know exactly when you're leaving," they replied. "If you want your passport, you have to pay for last year and this year."

Laci sighed. What could he do?

So he went home, paid his taxes, and returned with the fifty thousand crowns. He was expecting the price to have gone up even further by this point, but, to his surprise, the worker handed him three passports.

Laci thanked the worker, then made his way back home jubilantly to tell Olga the good news.

With passports and visas in hand, now all he needed were tickets for the ship. The problem was, those tickets could only be purchased in dollars, which he didn't have.

He turned to the Joint in Prague for help, and they offered him an exchange. He bought the tickets.

"Start packing," he told Olga as soon as he got home. "No jewelry, nothing. Leave everything here with your mother, we don't want to have any trouble at the border." At that time, he knew, you could only bring the equivalent of ten dollars per person outside of the country.

With one last look at their house, Laci and Olga said goodbye to Anna and her sisters. They promised they would send for them as soon as they could.

Evitchka sobbed into her grandmother's chest. "I'll miss you Babi," she wailed.

"I'll see you soon, child," Anna consoled her.

The little family then boarded the train for one last trip to Bratislava. They spent the night with Geza and Klara, and Geza accompanied them to the German border the next morning.

Before they reached the border, Laci handed Geza a pack with all of his gold and the few other possessions that were still on him. "Just keep it," he told him. "Thank you again for everything."

At the border, the Communist guards took them off the train and searched through all of their bags, patting them down to check their pockets. Olga's red lipstick in its silver tube? They took it. The guards seemed particularly intrigued by Laci's tallis, a prayer shawl, and tefillin, a set of small black leather boxes with leather straps containing scrolls of parchment inscribed with verses from the Torah. He had managed to keep these sacred items safe during the war. He left them there.

Finally, grudgingly, the guards allowed them to get back on the train. Before the train crossed the border, Geza prepared to disembark.

"Thank you, again," Laci said, shaking his hand one last time.

Geza leaned down closely to his ear. "After you cross the border, look under the seat in the third row," he whispered.

Before Laci could register what he was saying, he was gone.

The train crossed the border, and once they were safely in Germany, Laci did what he was told and looked under the seat. There, taped in a pouch, was the gold he had left with Geza.

When he showed it to Olga, she started to laugh. When Evitchka started nudging that she was hungry a short time later, Olga pulled a box of cookies out of her bag. To Laci's surprise, she started to break the cookies before handing little pieces to their daughter. Into her lap fell diamonds, rings and bracelets that had been baked inside.

"Aren't you clever?" he said, now laughing, too, as the train barreled on to Paris.

16

March 1949

On her last night in Paris before boarding a ship to America, seven-year-old Eva "Evitchka" Ritter encountered something she had never seen before — bananas.

She was taken in by their perfect complexion and the way they nearly dissolved in her mouth. So taken that she consumed approximately eight of them in one sitting.

She spent the next week aboard the Queen Elizabeth I regurgitating this delicacy, and she never ate bananas again.

That's how she remembers her life in America beginning.

There was a lot of excitement and nervous anticipation during those four-and-a-half days on the ship. Her parents celebrated their tenth wedding anniversary and talked about the life ahead of them.

"You should know, I'm prepared to work," she heard her mother tell her father, though her mother had never worked outside the home a day in her life.

She wondered what it would be like to be away from her mother. Other than the few hours a day she spent in school, they had never been apart.

Three of her aunts were there to greet them at the dock — Munci, who she couldn't wait to see, and Julia and Regina, her father's sisters who had come to America before the war and whom she had never met.

Eva became nervous as they approached, but her father was overcome with emotion to see his siblings. He truly hadn't known if he would ever see them again.

"My little Evitchka, oh how you've grown," said an excited Munci, embracing her in a big hug.

Eva nervously smiled at her other aunts, suddenly realizing how much her life was about to change.

Between the European immigrants and the American soldiers who had come home from war and settled down, apartments in New York were hard to come by. But Aunt Julia had a friend whose wife had just died, and the man agreed to rent them his Crown Heights apartment.

Eva didn't speak a word of English, but she started to pick up the language through weekly trips to the movies with her parents. It wasn't long before they enrolled her in a public school near her Aunt Julia's apartment. While learning her capitals, she correctly picked out though badly mispronounced "Dez Monnez, Iova," and the whole class laughed.

She took the trolley to school and had lunch at her aunt's house while her parents worked long hours. Her mother made good on her word and got a job in a relative's tie factory, turning ties from the wrong side on which they were sewn to the right side, day in and day out.

Her father, meanwhile, went to work with his brother-in-law Sam, Regina's husband, in a butcher shop. From the outset, Eva could tell he despised the business. He would come home filthy from breaking down chickens and cleaning slabs of meat, exhausted from haggling with the "yentas" over prices. Back home, he was the respected manager of two hundred employees. Here, he was the man behind the counter. By then, though, he was well used to putting one foot in front of the other.

A businessman at heart, he eventually scraped together enough money to buy his own kosher butcher shop, learning the ropes as he went.

Her parents saved just enough to enroll Eva at the Brooklyn Jewish Center. The school had refused them financial aid at first, but eventually relented. Eva knew it was important to her parents that she attend, though she wasn't quite sure why. After enrolling at the school, Eva came to find out it was important to her parents because her family was Jewish. This was something that had in hindsight been evident in practice at home in Humenné, but had never been openly called out, like the last name she had only recently become comfortable expressing.

After that first year, her grandmother Anna left Czechoslovakia and came to live with the family. Eva was so thrilled to see her Babi.

They shared a bedroom. Anna taught Eva to speak Hungarian in addition to her native Slovak and never talked about the war. She quickly claimed her place in the kitchen and cooked delicious meals while Eva's parents worked.

Though she was settling into her new life and doing well at school, Eva had trouble falling asleep at night. Her own memories of the war were hazy, but she would often hear her parents talking in hushed whispers. On the boat to America she had asked them, "We're going in the ocean. The Germans won't be able to come after us, right?"

Each night, she would convince Anna to lie awake waiting. "Don't go to sleep, Babi. I'm not asleep yet," she would call over from her twin bed.

When word got around to the family about Eva's sleeping troubles, her Uncle Sam from the butcher shop gave her a little prayer book that he got at a wedding. "If you put the prayer book under your pillow," he said, "you'll fall asleep with no trouble." For whatever reason, the method worked, and both Eva and Anna rested a little easier.

Eva continued to learn English at school, and her parents began to rely on her for lessons. But making friends was not easy. True or not, the family had the impression that there was a hierarchy amongst the Jews in New York, with those who had come from Germany years prior considering themselves "better" than the newer immigrants from Eastern Europe. Instead, most of their socializing took place amongst the extended family and recent immigrants from the old country. The families would gather in Prospect Park on Sundays, her father and Uncle Jack participating in weekly poker games, her mother socializing with her sisters-in-law and looking on while Eva played with her cousins.

This abundance of family was something she could not remember having back in Czechoslovakia; most of her relatives had either left the country before she did or died in the war.

On Fridays before Shabbat, her aunts and cousins would come by her apartment to pick up Anna's freshly baked challahs. Eva's Aunt Munci was often among them, with Eva's new baby cousin, Mark.

Settling in had not been easy for Munci. Her nerves were raw when she arrived in New York in 1946. She was afraid to cross the street or look at policemen. While staying with her sister in Rockaway, her niece's suitor threw a pebble at the window, and she thought there was a bombing.

Still, she desperately wanted to be independent. She enrolled in school to learn English and worked two nights a week sewing little dolls. A friend of her sister's was selling fur skins and said he would find Munci a job. She went to work making thirty five dollars a week, enough to cover the fifteen dollars in rent for her basement apartment and a can of peaches for dinner every now and then.

Seven months into school, she met Joseph Goldberg, who had been in the wholesale paper business back in Poland and had lost his entire family during the war. In America, he struggled to make ends meet, making twenty-six dollars a week.

Still, when he asked her to marry him, she was overjoyed. Their wedding took place on June 8, 1947, in Brooklyn, and their first son, Mark, was born two years later. Brother Steven soon followed.

Munci remained close with her brothers and their families, but she missed her parents desperately. As she thought about and planned for the life she wanted her children to have, her mother's last words to her were never far from her mind: never forget who you are.

Every Friday, her family lit Shabbat candles, and they kept a kosher home. When Mark was three, Munci and Joseph were walking together through the streets of Crown Heights when they came upon a schoolyard of Jewish children playing during recess time. What freedom, they thought. How lucky they were to be here.

Joseph turned his eyes heavenward and said to Munci, "God should only help me to be able to send my child to a yeshiva like this."

Through hard work and determination, his prayer was answered. Both Munci and Joseph worked two jobs to send their sons to yeshiva — a traditional Jewish educational institution focused on the study of Rabbinic literature — and Jewish summer camp. Munci told her children stories about the war and the family she had lost, and she made sure they knew how fortunate they were.

"Be good Jews. Keep the religion. Respect every religion," she taught them. "Be good citizens of America. Know that we suffered, but be happy with what you have."

17

February 1952

A few years after their arrival in America, the fibroid tumor that caused Olga to terminate her pregnancy during the war had returned. Her doctor told her she would again need surgery to remove it, and after the procedure, he approached her bed with a questioning look on his face.

"Who operated on you the first time?" he asked her.

"A German doctor in Czechoslovakia," she told him. "Why?"

"Because he cut through your fallopian tubes for no apparent reason. You won't be able to have more children."

Olga was taken aback. The doctor had told her she wouldn't be able to get pregnant again, but she thought it was because of a complication that couldn't be helped. In a perfect world, she would have loved to give Eva a brother or sister, as Jack and Roszi had done for little Judy with the arrival of a son after they came to America. Her doctor, a German, had been a Nazi, she now realized.

Germany had just begun to pay out reparations for Holocaust survivors. Laci and Anna were eligible for these benefits, as they were listed as survivors of concentration camps. Olga, having evaded capture, was not, despite the horrors she had endured on the outside.

Her doctor, looking to help her, sent her to a psychiatrist who was assessing Jews for psychological damage during the war.

"How do you feel about not being able to have more children?" he asked her.

She answered, stoically, "What you don't have, you don't miss." She did not qualify.

Laci, meanwhile, was doing everything he could to better their position in America while still supporting those who had helped him back home. As often as he could, he sent money to the Hajtases in Bratislava. He received postcards frequently from Jewish charitable organizations looking for support, and he gave what he could scrounge up.

After operating his own butcher shop for a few years, he sold the business and partnered with Sam in the wholesale delivery side of the industry. On most days, he left the house at 4:00 in the morning and returned at 10:00 at night. He spent hours on the road, day trips to Long Island or longer trips to Florida, delivering kosher meat, lifting forty-pound packages in and out of his truck. It was grueling, physical work, but he rarely complained.

Though frequently exhausted, he still found time to drive Eva to and from her dance lessons, often sitting outside and waiting for her to exit. A pre-teen by then, Eva had begun to attract the attention of boys — including one young man who worked in a fish shop near the dance school — and her father noticed, doing what he could to intercept a possible relationship.

By the time Eva had finished the eighth grade at the Brooklyn Jewish Center and enrolled at Midwood High School in Brooklyn, their Crown Heights neighborhood had begun to change. The family moved out to Kew Garden Hills in Queens, but Eva stayed at

Midwood using her cousin's address, where she was elected secretary of her class.

She began to date. Avram, who would pick her up in a different car each time; his father had a seat on the New York Stock Exchange. A boy by the last name of Romano. "Are you kidding?" her father asked when she told him about it. "He's Jewish," she reassured him.

Her senior year, she met Larry Rosenblatt. The two began dating, and it was serious.

She had also begun to plan her future. She had started volunteering at a hospital in Flushing and would have loved to study medicine, but ultimately she thought teaching would be a safer bet.

By the time she enrolled at Queens College in the fall in the education program, her courtship with Larry was serious. They had talked about getting engaged, but Larry seemed to get cold feet.

"Before we get engaged, let's make sure this is the right thing to do. Let's go out with other people," he told her.

Eva was devastated and angry. Despite her misgivings, she had turned down other suitors, imagining her life as the future Mrs. Rosenblatt. Truthfully, she had no desire to date anyone else.

Such was on her mind one beautiful spring afternoon of her freshman year when she was walking through the quad after her English class.

In the distance, she spied a young man — Michael, she thought his name was — who had asked her out a few weeks prior.

She said no at that time, but right now, she was ready to say yes to anybody just to make Larry jealous.

As he came closer, she lifted her hand to wave and then noticed the other man walking beside Michael, his dark hair and blue eyes catching her attention ever so slightly.

To her surprise, he glanced over at her at nearly the same time as she looked at him, and their eyes locked.

She held his gaze for just a moment, gave a small hint of a smile, and then kept walking.

Laci Ritter at his lumber yard in Radvan, circa 1937.

Laci and Olga Ritter, circa 1939.

Evitchka as a toddler, circa 1942.

A young Eva "Evitchka" Ritter after emigrating to America, circa 1949.

A teenage Eva Ritter with her father Laci, mother Olga and grandmother Anna in New York, circa 1959.

Larry Levitt and Eva Ritter at a summer camp in the Poconos, circa 1960.

Larry Levitt accepts the Jonas Salk Scholarship from Dr. Ralph J.
Bunche, United Nations Diplomat, 1961.

Larry and Eva Levitt on their wedding day, 1962.

Larry and Eva Levitt with their children, Adam, Marc and Lora, circa 1975.

Leonard Pool, founder of Air Products and Chemicals, who recruited Larry to Allentown to found a division of neurology at Lehigh Valley Hospital.

Geza and Klara Hajtas, the Catholic couple who risked their lives to save Eva and her mother, on a visit to the Levitt home in Allentown, 1987.

Larry and Eva Levitt, circa 2018.

PART 2

18

April 1960

"That's all for today," my professor said. "I'll see you next week."

I closed my book and stuffed my pencil and calculator into the front pocket of my backpack. Calculus was my favorite subject, and I knew how lucky I was to be learning from the best — my professor, Banesh Hoffman, had worked with Albert Einstein, after all.

As I took off down the stairs and out the building's front doors, I spotted my long-time friend Michael Olman a few paces ahead.

"Hey, Michael!" I quickly strode to catch up with him.

"Hi Larry," Michael said, not at all surprised to see me. His Tuesday afternoon class was in the same building, and we frequently ran into each other.

"Are we meeting up to study tonight?" I asked him. "Or do you have a date with that girl you've been telling me about?"

"I asked her out two weeks ago, but she turned me down for the third time," Michael said dejectedly. "Said she's got a boyfriend, and I guess it's serious."

"Sorry to hear that," I said. "You'll just have to go after another one of Queens College's finest."

We walked through campus, me heading to the library and Michael to his next class. We were about to part ways when Michael grabbed my shoulder and gestured subtly across the quad.

"Don't look now, but there she is," he said in a low tone.

Of course I had to look. I craned my neck in the direction of his gesture and saw a girl with lightly tanned skin and a bobbing blond ponytail walking on the opposite side of the path. As she came closer, Michael lifted his hand in a quick wave, and she raised hers in return. Her head then turned ever so slightly in my direction, and we locked eyes for just a second before she looked away. As she kept walking, my eyes followed her until she was out of my peripheral vision.

"Wow, she really is beautiful," I said to Michael once she was out of ear shot.

"I know, what did I tell you!" he said.

"Mind if I give it a try?" I asked him.

"I guess it's okay," he said, "though I doubt you'll have better luck."

The following Tuesday, I made a point to lose Michael in the crowd after calculus. I took the steps two at a time and hurried to the quad, catching my breath as I lingered awkwardly on the path where I had first spotted her. Would this work? Would she be here?

After what felt like an hour of shifting from one foot to the other and pretending to study my calculus notes, I spotted her coming toward me. I began walking slowly to meet her halfway.

"Hello!" I said abruptly as we came face to face. "I'm a friend of Michael Olman's. He's told me many nice things about you, and I wanted to meet you."

I knew I was rambling, but I couldn't stop myself. She was even more beautiful up close with her big green eyes and whisps of blond hair bordering her face.

"Well, it's nice to meet you," she said politely. "I'm Eva."

"Larry," I said, reaching out to shake her hand. I noticed her twinge just a little at the mention of my name.

"Eva, would you consider going out with me tonight?" I asked nervously. "There's a new movie playing at the cineplex that we could go see."

A beat of silence passed. I fidgeted again, sure I was about to be rejected like Michael.

"Yes, I will go out with you," she answered after what felt like an eternity.

Stunned, it took me a moment to gather myself to answer back.

"Wonderful!" I said.

"Will you write your address?" I asked, quickly pulling out my calculus notebook and flipping to a half-blank page before handing it to her along with a pencil.

She took the paper and pencil and hastily scribbled her address in Queens before handing it back to me.

"Wonderful," I said again. "I'll pick you up at seven."

I took the Q 44 bus the hour and a half back to the Bronx after my next class to ask my father if I could borrow his car. If it were one of my three older sisters asking, he likely would have hesitated, but for me, the baby and his only son, it was anything goes.

I drove back to Queens in my father's old Pontiac, navigating the streets I knew well until I found her address. I parked the car at the curb in front of the brownstone in Kew Garden Hills, timidly walked up the steps, and knocked on the front door. A dark-haired woman with blue eyes opened it.

"Hello, can I help you?" the woman asked in her thick European accent.

"Hello, Ma'am. I'm Larry Levitt. I'm here to pick up your daughter."

Just then, Eva brushed past her mother through the doorway and, with a wave, we set off.

"Don't worry, Anu, we won't be late," she called over her shoulder.

We made small talk on the short ride to the movie theater. I found out she was a first-year student studying education. I told her of my hopes of becoming a doctor, though as I was only in my third year at Queens, it felt a long way off.

We parked the car near the theater, walked the block or so over, and approached the window.

"Two tickets for 'Flower Drum Song,'" I said to the teenager working the ticket booth.

I slid two dollar bills underneath the glass window, and he pushed back my change and the tickets. Once inside, I doled out another ten cents for popcorn and two small sodas, and then we found our seats.

I settled comfortably into mine, but Eva seemed to contort herself against the furthest armrest, stretching her arm at nearly full length to reach the popcorn. She stared intently at the screen as the movie began, and while my eyes kept wandering toward hers, she refused to meet my gaze.

Two hours later, our popcorn and sodas long gone, the lights came up in the theater. I stood, stretching my arms above my head. Eva quickly grabbed her coat, tossing it over her shoulders and putting her arms through.

"Would you care to take a walk?" I asked her on the way out, not ready for the evening to end.

"Would you please just take me home?" she asked quietly.

"Yes, I can take you home," I said, failing miserably to hide my disappointment. We rode in near silence before I dropped her off in front of her house, certain not to hear from her again.

The next morning, I was surprised when my sister Miriam yelled that there was a girl on the phone for me.

"Hello," I said uncertainly, picking up the receiver from the kitchen wall.

"Larry," the voice on the other end said. "It's Eva."

"Oh, hi, Eva. Is everything okay? Did you leave something in my car?" I asked.

"No, I'm calling to apologize for how I treated you last night. It was very rude of me to end our date like that," she said.

"Oh, that's okay. I understand if you weren't having a good time," I said, though I didn't quite understand as I was having a lovely time up until that point.

"It's not that," she said. "You were very sweet, but I've been seeing someone for a while, about a year and a half. His name also happens to be Larry. I thought he was going to propose, but just this past week he told me we should see other people, and then here you come along and ask me out, so I said yes. So, it's not your fault at all. You're just not the other Larry."

The pieces came together in my head as I formulated my response. She didn't prefer me over Michael, my timing was just better. Or was it?

"I accept your apology," I said, though the wheels had already started spinning in my head. What did I have to lose? "However," I went on, "if you're willing, I'd say the best way to make it up to me would be a do-over. Are you free Saturday night?"

Though it was probably just her sense of duty and politeness rather than a true desire, she said, "Yes, I will see you Saturday."

Our second date went much better than the first, and dare I say she even forgot about the other Larry. Before long, we were spending most of our free time on campus together and our nights deep in conversation on the telephone. Sometimes, I could hear her father speaking Slovak in the background, or her grandmother in her Hungarian accent. My own parents' Yiddish would sometimes reach her ears. I became a frequent guest at Shabbat dinner with her family.

Each time I saw Michael walking out of calculus after that, he dodged my advances and took off in the other direction.

I was at her house one Friday afternoon, her mother and grandmother busily cooking in the kitchen, when the doorbell rang. I watched as her mother quickly wiped her hands on her apron and hurried down the hall to open the door. I looked on curiously from the kitchen and saw an older couple that I didn't recognize step into the foyer. Based on their conversation, it soon became clear that these were the other Larry's parents.

"Please, Olga, he made a mistake," I heard the woman say, her voice catching in her throat. "He's ready now, he will buy her an engagement ring." Then, in a hushed tone, "I know she's seeing someone, but if she doesn't say yes to my Larry, I don't know what he'll do."

"Please, ask your daughter to give my son another chance," the other Larry's father pleaded with Eva's father, Laci, who had joined his wife at the door.

"She doesn't want to get married. What can I do?" her father said.

With a deep sigh, the other Larry's mother turned around and walked out the door, his father following sheepishly behind.

When they left, Eva turned to me to quickly apologize.

"I thought I wanted to marry him, but after we got together I realized I could never truly be myself with the other Larry. He was always so critical, and I just felt so insecure. I was afraid to even get up to dance when I was with him," she said. Then she leaned in to give me a kiss on the cheek. "You're the only Larry for me," she declared.

19

June 1961

We both continued our studies at Queens College, and when I was awarded the coveted Jonas Salk scholarship to study medicine at the Weill Cornell Medical School, Eva was there to cheer me on as Ralph Bunche, a United Nations diplomat for twenty-five years and the 1950 recipient of the Nobel Peace Prize, shook my hand.

I began my studies at Cornell that fall and moved into Olin Hall, the dorm for single students on 69th Street and York Avenue in Manhattan. My plans to become a doctor, however, nearly derailed as quickly as they began.

I was a good student, I had graduated first in my premed class, after all, but there was one course I just couldn't handle — anatomy. No matter how hard I tried, I couldn't visualize the relationships between the organs that I was dissecting and the veins and arteries going into those organs.

Professor Roy Swan, who would make rounds in the dissection laboratory, used to bark at me, "Levitt, what's the relationship between the pancreas and the pancreatic artery?" and I just couldn't remember.

No matter how long I studied the night before, I couldn't answer his questions. The other guys at my table, Morton, a star student, Jerry, who used to work in a morgue, and Lance, who had a photographic memory, would always know the answers right away.

One day, I was called down to the office of Dean Lawrence Hanlon. He said, "Levitt, what's wrong with you? You're doing well in all the other subjects, but you can't do anatomy? You're going to have to pass anatomy or you can't go on to the second year."

The dean sent me to the Payne-Whitney Clinic, one of the most famous psychiatric hospitals in New York, where one of the senior psychiatrists made me lie down on a couch in his office. He asked me about my mother, my father, memories from my early years, even toilet training.

A few weeks later, Dean Hanlon called me down to his office again. "Levitt, how are you doing there at the Payne-Whitney Clinic?"

"I think I'm doing okay," I said, "but I'm not doing any better in anatomy."

"I have another idea," he said. "Go talk to Alex Reeves, one of our fourth-year students. He's really good at anatomy, maybe he can help you."

So I went to see Alex. "How are you studying?" he asked me.

"I look at the two textbooks, *Grant's Atlas* and *Cunningham's Textbook of Anatomy*, the night before, and then I dissect the cadaver and when Dr. Swan asks me questions, I can't answer them. Alex, I don't know why," I said.

"I have an idea for you Larry," he said. "Instead of looking at the pictures in the book the night before and then cutting up the cadaver, I want you to do it backwards. I want you to work on the cadaver and then study what you learned the night after."

The next anatomy lab, I tried what he said, and the next time Professor Roy Swan asked me a question, I even surprised myself with the right answer.

"Eva, I won't have to go to pharmacy school after all," I told her one Friday night, much to the relief of her parents, who were thrilled beyond measure that their daughter was dating a Jewish soon-to-be doctor.

"I knew you could do it all along," she said.

Not long after I finished my first year of medical school, I asked Eva to become my wife. I had known from the first moment I saw her that I would, if given the chance.

Though our relationship was solid, I was still nervous. What would she say? Having grown close to her parents over the intervening months, I approached them with my concerns.

"Larry," Olga said in her thick accent, "you never get anything if you don't ask."

She left the room for a moment as I sat there mulling this over. When she returned, she took my hand, turned it over, and placed something small and solid into my open palm

"Give this to my Evitchka," she said proudly.

When I looked down, I noticed the empty space on Olga's finger. Knowing I was just a poor kid from the Bronx working his way through medical school, she had given me her own engagement ring.

We were married a year later, on June 10, 1962, at the Young Israel Synagogue in Queens. When Rabbi Fabian Schonfeld announced, "I now pronounce you man and wife," I leaned over to kiss my beautiful Eva under the chuppah, despite the rabbi's attempts to stop us — it wasn't the orthodox way.

The reception was held at a nearby social hall with two hundred guests in attendance. My sisters were there with their husbands and children, Eva's parents and grandmother, her aunts, uncles, and cousins.

At one point, my parents were called to the dance floor for a traditional dance called the *mezinka* — only performed when the last child in your family marries. They sat proudly in the center as Eva and I placed crowns on their heads, and the rest of the family danced around them with brooms.

Then it was her parents' turn for the *mezinka*. Eva, of course, was their last child to marry, but also their first and their only, atypical for a Jewish family and, from what I came to know, not by design.

I thought I knew then how lucky I was to have her, but it would take years for me to truly understand how many acts of fate, luck, and perseverance it took for Eva and me to start our lives together.

20

October 1962

I crouched beneath the hanging coats and pulled the accordion door shut. It was almost 5:00 p.m., and I waited wildly for the sound of a key turning in the lock. Finally, there was a creak, and I heard the door open. That was my cue. Out I sprang from the closet, only steps away from the door in our miniscule studio apartment on 69th and York. Eva let out a scream of terror and pleasure all at once, followed by a breathless giggle as I moved to embrace her. Got her again, I thought.

This near nightly routine had led to questions from neighbors more than once if Eva was having nightmares from the war.

"How was your day?" I asked her, already anticipating the answer.

"Oh, it was awful, as usual," said Eva, though with a hint of a sarcastic smile. "You wouldn't believe it...today we saw a mouse running through the hall, and I slammed the door shut right on it. The kids were very well behaved for the rest of the day, wouldn't you know."

"Wow! What did Mrs. Waltzer say?" I asked. I knew the feisty, white-haired woman serving as the principal at P.S. 118 in Harlem would have wanted to weigh in.

"She said if I could handle those kids plus a mouse, maybe she won't need to give me a better class next year after all."

"But she promised! If you make it through the year that is," I said.

"Oh, I'll make it," Eva said. She was the eighth and most determined teacher that third grade class had ever had.

"You have class tonight?" I asked. Eva had graduated early from Queens College and was supporting us on her teacher's salary while also studying for her master's in education, while I worked my way through medical school.

"Not tonight. We're going out with the Rothmans, remember?" she said.

"How could I forget!" I said, though I knew how, as I was perpetually exhausted from studying and clinical work. I had just finished my obstetrics rotation and was about to start neurology, for which I was particularly excited.

We grabbed our coats and headed out to meet Lew and Anne and Lew's parents at the Hungarian restaurant on 1st Avenue. Lew's father Herman was a well-known internist in New York and would be treating two med students and two young teachers to dinner. It was the highlight of our month, as most of our meals consisted of whatever we could scrape together.

Eva indeed made it through that first year in Harlem and was rewarded with a better behaved third grade class the following year.

She never stopped trying to help her students. One day, she saw that the Goodyear Rubber Company was providing free boots to kids in need. She wrote to the company, and her whole class got free boots.

I'm not sure what it was exactly that lured the young Eva to one particular student, Jimmy, but one Friday afternoon, she asked his mother if she could take him home with her for the weekend. "Whatever you want," his mother said.

124

So, Jimmy rode with us from Manhattan to Queens for Shabbat dinner at Eva's parents' house. Her parents welcomed him with open arms. Her grandmother Anna was, however, not happy that she had brought someone not Jewish to Shabbat, and she refused to come out of her room for the entire meal.

Jimmy slurped his matzah ball soup and had three helpings of brisket. After dinner, Eva gave him a bath, and we put him to bed in one of the spare bedrooms.

Saturday morning around 10:00, we still hadn't heard a word from him. We opened the door and peeked in to make sure he was breathing. Same thing at eleven. By twelve, we began to worry and went to wake him. He startled, but then his face relaxed again.

"*La cama es suave,*" he said in Spanish, the bed is soft, then in broken English, "I've never slept in my own bed before."

When the weekend was over, Eva and I drove him back to his apartment in Harlem. We caught a glimpse of his living conditions before giving him a hug and saying goodbye.

"*Gracias,*" he said, and walked away.

21

February 1965

It was a rare evening home together. We had just finished dinner, and I was making coffee when the phone rang. It was Eva's mother.

I could see the worried look on Eva's face as she peppered her mother with questions, but I couldn't quite catch the gist of the issue from a single side of the conversation. Then Eva handed the phone to me. "Larry, Anu wants your advice."

Though I was only in my fourth year of medical school by that time, they already considered me the doctor in the family. I knew whatever she wanted advice about was not going to be good.

"What's wrong?" I asked, taking the phone from Eva and stretching the cord across the table.

"It's Babi," she said, using the Hungarian word for grandmother. "She's lighting the Shabbat candles."

This didn't seem too perplexing at first. After all, Eva's grandmother had lit the traditional Shabbat candles in her family's silver candelabra every Friday since I had known her. Then, I realized it was Wednesday.

"Is anything else bothering her?" I asked, increasingly alarmed.

"She does say she has a headache all of a sudden, and she feels warm to me," Olga said.

I wasn't sure what was wrong, but I had a feeling there was something truly amiss. "Call an ambulance," I told her. "Have them take her to The New York Hospital Emergency Room."

When I hung up the phone, I quickly called the ER to let them know about her imminent arrival. Then Eva and I grabbed our coats and walked across the street to the hospital to wait outside the emergency entrance.

When the ambulance finally arrived after what felt like forever, the doors swung open and out came a gurney carrying Eva's beloved Babi. I could see an angry red rash across her face.

We followed her inside, but we were turned away as a curtain was pulled around her bed. "Would you mind waiting out here?" the doctor asked, motioning Eva's mother to come with him. "We'll update you as soon as we know something."

Eva's father soon arrived — having found a note in the kitchen when he returned from work hastily scribbled by his wife — and we filled him in on what we knew.

I tried to make out the murmurs through the curtain, but I couldn't glean too much. Finally, after a long half hour, Dr. Parker and a young intern, Dr. Weld, emerged from the curtain, accompanied by Olga.

"We're not sure what's wrong, but her condition is clearly critical," Dr. Parker said. Anna Roth had a fever of 105, a total body rash, and a dangerously low blood pressure, he reported. "We need to admit her to the ICU right away."

Shortly after she was taken to the Intensive Care Unit, the attending physician arrived to examine her. "Her fever is still high," he reported briskly. He said she had also suffered a stroke which had paralyzed her left side, and her EKG was abnormal, which meant she might have suffered a heart attack as well.

"Such an overwhelming combination of problems in a sixty-five-year-old lady is unlikely to be treatable," he said matter-of-factly. "I'd suggest you all go home to get some sleep. Her doctors will let you know if anything happens or when it's over."

Eva's face went white. Her mother leaned on Laci's shoulder, burying her head in his jacket. We all knew what the doctor was saying.

Her caretakers huddled for a minute, and then Dr. Parker and the nurse walked out. Dr. Weld, who looked about my age, turned to us before he left.

"I'm not sure why your mother is so sick," he said to Olga. "But I don't plan to give up until I'm absolutely certain that she can't recover."

We sat numbly in the ICU waiting room for several hours, not ready to leave, even on the doctor's orders. Each time we saw Dr. Weld emerge through the double doors, we rushed over to ask for an update.

At one point, he told us that she had lapsed into a coma. Later, he said that they had decided to put her on a broad-spectrum antibiotic because it was possible she had some sort of overwhelming infection. They'd also given her medication to raise her blood pressure. And they'd performed a series of blood tests and sent them off to the lab.

By midnight, we were all exhausted, and Eva and I decided it was time to walk back to our apartment to get some sleep. Her parents insisted on staying.

We walked up the stairs to the second floor, unlocking our door and tossing our coats on the table, too tired to bother hanging them up. We pulled the couch out into its bed-like form and tucked ourselves under the covers. But neither of us could sleep. Eva stared at the ceiling while I tossed and turned, thinking of her grandmother alone in that bed and how I couldn't do anything to help.

After an hour or two, I couldn't take it anymore. I quietly dressed in the dark, pulled on my coat, and whispered to Eva that I was going to check on her Babi.

I made my way back across the street and through the hospital's winding, brightly lit halls to the ICU waiting room. I found my mother-in-law curled up on a couch and my father-in-law stretched out in a lounge chair. They reported that they had gone in to see Anna twice since we'd left, both times finding her unresponsive and her breathing labored.

Then there was Dr. Weld, again coming out to the waiting room. Was this the news we had been dreading?

"Anna is doing a bit better," he said to all of our surprise. Her temperature was down to 103, and her blood pressure was back up to 100, he said. Her spinal tap had come back normal.

"We may not know what's wrong with her for a while," he said, noting the results of the blood test could take weeks. "But I'm cautiously optimistic."

Over the next week, she did indeed begin to slowly improve. She began to move her limbs and then to speak, though in a mumbled tone. Then one evening, we were stunned upon entering her room to see her sitting in a chair next to the bed.

"Babi!" Eva exclaimed. "How are you?"

"Little better, Evitchka," she said, reaching out her hand toward Eva, who grasped it with both of her hands, looking like she had witnessed a miracle.

Dr. Weld came in then. "Her temperature is normal and her pulse and blood pressure are now stable," he said with a smile. "We hope to get her walking soon."

With the help of physical therapy, she was walking with a cane three days later. She was starting to speak in longer, clearer phrases. Twelve days after her hospital admission, she was released to a rehabilitation facility. Two weeks after that and with steady improvement, she was able to come home.

Another two weeks later, I found a message in my student mailbox that Dr. Weld wanted to speak with me.

"Larry," he said, meeting me outside of the ICU later that day, "we seem to have solved the case of your wife's grandmother."

The results of the blood test came back, he said. Anna was suffering from Brill's disease.

Brill's disease, he explained, was a form of recurring typhus that could show up years — even decades — after an infection. Her symptoms had presented like typhus, and though they didn't have an official diagnosis, the antibiotic chloramphenicol that Dr. Weld had added on after his middle-of-the-night research had effectively treated the disease.

"Do you know how she might have contracted typhus?" Dr. Weld asked curiously.

Having heard the stories for many years now from my wife and her family, I did know. I told Dr. Weld about the time Anna Roth spent in Auschwitz.

22

July 1965

I cradled the phone to my ear and dialed my wife. I could picture her washing the dishes after her dinner for one in our new two-bedroom apartment in nearby Stuyvesant town.

"How's it going?" Eva asked anxiously.

"Oh, everything's fine here," I lied, clearly unable to hide the discouragement in my voice after a harrowing first day as an intern at Bellevue Hospital in the Cornell Division. Running through my mind was the old adage, "Don't get admitted to a hospital in July as many of the doctors are new."

We chatted for a few minutes as I told her about a patient named Mrs. Reilly and how I found her that morning lying listlessly on a cot in the crowded emergency room, thin and pale, her blood pressure low, her pulse rapid.

As I approached the bed, she gestured for me to lower my head toward her as she spoke out hoarsely in her Irish drawl, "Dr. Levitt, I think I'm going to die."

"Now, now, I promise you, we won't let that happen," I reassured her, with all of the confidence of a first-year intern on his very first day on the job.

I ran all the tests I could think of, all the while managing the other dozen patients assigned to me, plus anything new that came in. As I was drawing blood for a routine crossmatch, Mrs. Reilly's pressure suddenly dropped precipitously.

"My chest hurts!" she cried out. Within seconds, she went into shock and became unresponsive. I tried to resuscitate her, but it was too late.

"Deep down, I know I did everything I could," I told Eva, "yet I brushed aside her worries at the seriousness of her condition. How will I ever learn to help such a patient?"

"Trust your instincts, Larry. I know you can do it," she reassured me before we hung up.

It was the fuel I needed to keep going.

The next few hours were a blur of activity, but I was managing, until I noticed my co-interns signing out that evening, leaving me responsible for all thirty-six patients on Ground B, the women's ward, until the following morning. I ran from patient to patient and, around 1:00 in the morning, I heard a staticky voice bellow over the loudspeaker, "Dr. Levitt to the ER, stat!"

I took the stairs two at a time up to the ER where I found my new patient, Mrs. Goldberg, a plump, seventy-five-year-old woman, wearing a necklace with a Jewish star and sweating profusely. I immediately thought of my own mother who so proudly referred to me as "my son, the doctor." I doubted whether she'd feel proud of me that day.

Mrs. Goldberg had a high fever, a full body rash, and a bad headache. I suspected meningitis and performed a lumbar puncture to confirm my suspicion, starting her on antibiotics while I waited on the results. I checked on her constantly throughout the night, worried I would lose another patient on my first day.

Thankfully, she made it through the night. I did too, but just barely. By morning, I was so exhausted, I could hardly stand. And I knew it would be another twelve hours before I could get any rest.

Finally, at 6:30 that evening, I burst through the hospital doors and began the short walk to our apartment, breathing in the muggy, sticky, New York summer air and enjoying every second of it.

When I arrived home, Eva had my favorite dinner on the table. As I savored every bite of her roast chicken and baked potatoes, I began to tell her more about the events of the last thirty-six hours, but after a few minutes, I stopped talking. I had fallen asleep at the dinner table.

By 6:45 the next morning, I was gulping down breakfast and racing back to the hospital. I was more anxious than ever, but I did the best I could over the next two days. Then, on the following night, when I was again on call, Mrs. Harris arrived at the emergency room at 3:00 in the morning. She was sixty-six years old and looking fairly healthy, but after complaining of chest pains, her husband had convinced her to go to the emergency room. An EKG showed she had a small heart attack, so we admitted her.

I was writing up my notes in her chart when I heard a nurse yell "Code Blue, cardiac arrest, bed 14, stat." I raced back to Mrs. Harris' bedside and immediately began CPR. Two minutes later, the code blue team arrived and took over, but after ten minutes of nonstop efforts, the team decided there was nothing more they could do. Time of death, 4:03 a.m.

For the second time that week, I had to walk out to the waiting room and inform loved ones of a family member's unexpected death. I witnessed their shock and pain and felt guilty and responsible. As night turned to morning and reinforcements mercifully started to file in, I turned around and headed straight for the office of Dr. Lawrence

Scherr, director of programs for interns and residents at Cornell-Bellevue.

After a few minutes' wait, his secretary led me into his wood-paneled office. Dr. Scherr, a tall, striking man with a sharp nose and prominent jaw, looked up from his desk and invited me to sit down.

"Larry, what can I do for you?" he asked briskly.

I took a deep breath. "Dr. Scherr, I'm really sorry to bother you, but I've had an awful first few days."

He said nothing, so I continued.

"Two patients of mine have died. I've hardly slept, and I feel upset way too much of the time," I went on. "I really don't think I'm cut out to be a doctor."

I looked down, gathering courage for what I was about to say, and then looked up to meet his gaze.

"I'm very, very sorry to disappoint you, but I've decided to resign."

Dr. Scherr looked nonplused. "Larry, you're the fourth intern who has come down to see me this week with a similar story. Look, I know you can do it. Just do the very best you can. Now turn around and get back to work."

I was stunned. "Okay, I'll try," I said meekly, and turned around and left his office.

Walking back down to the ER, I ran into my friend Lew Rothman, who had also just started interning at Bellevue through Columbia while I was part of the Cornell division.

"I'm dying over here, but I see you're all smiles...what's up?" I asked him quizzically.

"I'm on Librium," he said, referencing the anti-anxiety drug that seemed to have lightened his mood, and continued on his way.

When my shift finally ended, I made my way home to relay the day's events to Eva, who was exhausted from her own long day of teaching in Harlem.

"Dr. Scherr is right, darling, I know you can do it," she said confidently, leaning over to kiss me on the cheek.

I breathed a deep sigh of relief and fell asleep with my clothes on in our bed.

23

January 1966

The next few months passed in a blur of long, grueling shifts, weekends on call, and sparingly little sleep. I hardly noticed as Eva's midsection began to grow rounder, her feet more swollen. It was easy to miss her pregnancy, really, as she never complained, not even once.

On one of our nightly check-in calls from the hospital in late January, Eva reported that she had been to see her obstetrician.

"I told him this baby is past its due date, but he said I'm being silly, and I'll go into labor when it's time," she said.

"Oh, he's probably right," I told her, my mind already wandering to my next patient. "Just wait it out, and everything will be fine."

By her calculation, she was already one month past her due date when she eventually persuaded her obstetrician to induce labor on February 9.

I could have asked for the day off, but as a twenty-five-year-old intern, I was afraid of the implications.

"Won't your mother go with you?" I asked before I left the house that morning.

"With everything she's been through?" she replied. "I couldn't live with myself if I caused her any more stress. I'll call her afterward."

It was a familiar refrain from Eva, who was fiercely protective of her parents and their feelings.

So off I went to work while Eva took a cab uptown by herself to The New York Hospital.

Hours later, while I was admitting a patient with pneumonia from the emergency room, I got a call from Dr. Langer, Eva's obstetrician.

"Hello!" I said excitedly, grabbing for the phone, anxious for the news.

"Dr. Levitt, I want you to know that your wife has just given birth to a baby boy," he said in an odd monotone.

"That's wonderful!" I exclaimed back. Our son, who we had already decided to name Adam, was finally here.

Then, his voice turned tense and strained, and he said, "Dr. Levitt, Adam is having convulsions and you need to come to the hospital immediately."

I was stunned, and I told Dr. Langer I would be there as soon as I possibly could.

Shaking, I quickly got coverage from a colleague, ran into the snowy morning, and jumped into a cab. When I got to the hospital, I found Eva in her room sitting up in bed, pale, groggy, and tearful. "Oh my God," she sobbed, "I can't believe this is happening." She managed to tell me that a pediatrician was in the nursery treating Adam for his convulsions.

Rushing there, I saw a tiny, blond-haired infant seizing in the pediatric intensive care unit, surrounded by doctors and nurses. After what seemed like an eternity but was probably only fifteen or twenty seconds, Adam's seizure stopped. A tall, thin, gray-haired gentleman came over to talk to me. He was Dr. Altman, the pediatric intensive care specialist. He told me that Adam had suffered birth anoxia — lack of oxygen — because the umbilical cord had been wrapped around his neck. The lack of oxygen had, in turn, caused the seizures.

Adam's brain had been injured and his left side was obviously weak. His probable diagnosis — cerebral palsy.

My heart fell into my stomach. "I'm sorry," Dr. Altman said in a matter-of-fact, not particularly sympathetic voice. He turned and left, and I stood alone, hardly breathing, struggling to take in the reality that mine and Eva's lives had just changed forever.

Later that day, as I peered in at Adam, lying there helpless in his incubator, I noticed his long fingernails — the sign of a baby born well overdue. That additional time likely led to the umbilical cord problem, leading to the lack of oxygen, I realized sadly.

Adam left the hospital after two weeks, and when the nurse handed the bundled-up baby to Eva, the reality of the change in our lives really sunk in.

While I continued to spend most of my nights at the hospital, Eva was alone with Adam. She hardly slept, woken several times a night to feed and diaper and swaddle him. I could see the stress this placed on her, and could only offer emotional support, as my physical energy was devoted to work.

After a few months, I could tell she was starting to go stir crazy. I encouraged her to hire a weekly babysitter, and she went back to substitute teaching in Harlem on Wednesdays. The money was negligible, but the time out of the house was invaluable.

On Fridays, her father would pick her and Adam up and take them to Queens to spend the weekend during my call shifts.

"Will you let your parents watch him for an hour or two this weekend and take a break?" I asked hopefully on one of my rare evenings at home. She had managed to make dinner, and was bouncing the baby on her hip with a gentle shushing tone so I could eat in peace.

"I'll think about it," she said, and while I knew how much her parents loved their grandson and wanted to help, she probably wouldn't ask. She didn't want to be a burden.

Adam wasn't meeting his milestones, but our pediatrician continued to assure us that everything was fine. I thought about the other young doctors in the hospital whose wives had recently given birth. They passed around photos of their healthy children with obvious pleasure, announcing their child's latest accomplishments with pride. I tried to be happy for them, but privately, I felt shattered.

Still, despite the challenges we were facing with Adam, we were considering expanding our family.

Of course we worried. Could we bear having another child with special needs? Several physicians reassured us that what happened to Adam was unlikely to recur. And, knowing what her parents had sacrificed, Eva had always wanted a big family. And so, with some trepidation, we decided to try to have another baby.

By fall, I had started my residency, a combined program at Bellevue and Memorial Sloan Kettering. Eva, once again, was pregnant.

24

January 1967

A grainy tone over the loudspeaker at Bellevue said, "Dr. Levitt, call for you on line one. Levitt, line one."

Had something happened to Adam? He was eleven months old and still unable to sit up on his own, which deep down I knew was a likely harbinger of future troubles. He and Eva were with her parents in Queens, and I knew she wouldn't call unless something was truly wrong.

"A nurse will be right over to check on you," I told my patient, hurriedly pulling the curtain closed around her bed.

As I rushed down the hall to the admittance desk, I glanced out the window and noticed that dusk had settled in.

"Hello, this is Dr. Levitt."

"Larry? This is Saul Rosenfeld, from your parents' synagogue in the Bronx. I'm sorry, but I'm calling with some bad news." His name sounded vaguely familiar, but I couldn't quite place it. Perhaps we had met at holiday services? I could hear the hesitancy in his voice and waited as he paused for a moment. "Your father died this morning."

I sucked in a breath and the receiver nearly fell from my hand. My mind immediately flashed to my conversation with my father from earlier that week. He told me he was having palpitations in his chest. After his mild heart attack a few months back, the complaint did worry me, and I advised him to speak to his doctor, but I didn't check to see if he followed through.

"Where is he?" I asked, already feeling myself falling into a daze. "What happened?"

"He came into the synagogue, put on his tallis, and just dropped dead," Saul said, the sadness evident in his voice at both the occurrence and having to endure this conversation. "We couldn't move him until the end of Shabbos. He's still here, waiting for the coroner."

"I'll be right over," I said, and with a hurried explanation to the charge nurse to reassign my patients, I took off into the cold January night to catch the bus to the Bronx. On the way, I thought about how Morris Levitt had been lucky enough to emigrate to the United States from Ukraine in the 1920s, after the first World War but before the second. How fortunate we both were that he had met my mother, Esther Kaufman, who had come to America from the same small town of Mohyliv-Podilskyi with her parents at the age of sixteen. He found satisfaction in the fur business all these years, even though he sewed fur skins together on the same sewing machine for decades.

When I arrived, I found my father lying there in the aisle, his prayer shawl draped over him. My mother sat crying in a nearby pew.

"It'll be okay, Mommy," I said, moving to console her. "I'll take care of everything."

While I made the arrangements for the funeral, Eva made the arrangements for me. She looked after Adam and made sure I ate proper meals and got at least some sleep.

We sat shiva at my parents' apartment over the next week. Spending all that time in the Bronx brought me right back to my days of playing stickball on Leydig Avenue, where I had become known as a "two-sewer man" thanks to my prowess of hitting the stickball two sewer lengths. I took pride in the moniker — Willie Mays was a three-sewer man, and he became a famous baseball player.

Eva, her mother, and her grandmother kept themselves busy in the kitchen so my sisters, my mother, and I could receive visitors and share memories. Each night, we recited the mourners' kaddish together.

The week passed in a blur and, too soon, it was back to work. In my final months at Bellevue, I began to take an interest in neurology. Perhaps my experience at home with Adam was leading me in that direction. I overanalyzed each night why he wasn't crawling, standing, or talking as his first birthday came and went.

With my recent loss still weighing heavily on my mind, I began the final four-month rotation of my first-year residency at the Memorial Sloan Kettering Cancer Center. Complicated cases were a good distraction, and there was no shortage of them at Memorial Sloan Kettering. Patients traveled with their families from all over the country to be treated there. That winter, Mrs. Dorothy Pool was one of them.

Mrs. Pool had recently been diagnosed with lung cancer, but she had been managing fairly well. When she suddenly fell into an extremely weak state out of nowhere, her doctors in her home town of Allentown, Pennsylvania, couldn't figure out the cause. At a loss, they advised her husband, Leonard, to bring her to Memorial Sloan Kettering.

I was assigned to the case, along with my attending physician, Dr. William Geller. As I examined Mrs. Pool — a gray-haired woman lying frail and motionless, unable to utter more than two words at a time — I could feel her husband's eyes following my every move from his chair across from the bed. My age was evident, along with the inexperience that came with it.

"Dr. Levitt?" Mr. Pool said when I had completed my exam. "Could we talk a moment?"

I sat down apprehensively in the green vinyl chair opposite a man who appeared to be in his sixties, wearing corduroys and a plaid flannel shirt. I prepared myself to be peppered with questions about causes, treatment options, and potential outcomes, the answers to which I didn't yet have. But instead he just said, "It's good of you to help us."

He told me that Dorothy had received her diagnosis of lung cancer earlier that year, after three decades of chain smoking. "I tried to get her to stop, but ..." he trailed off. After a round of radiation, she had recovered some of her energy. She'd been going out with friends, taking scenic walks, even traveling to visit her sister in Detroit.

"Two weeks ago, she just became so exhausted, as if all the energy had been scooped out of her," Mr. Pool said. "She got so weak, she could barely stand."

I could tell how much he adored his wife — a feeling I knew well — and felt the weight of that responsibility crushing down on me, at twenty-seven years old, barely a doctor. I wanted to diagnose and treat her and send her happily home to Allentown with her husband. I also wanted to run out of the room and hide.

"You'll help us?" he asked, a mix of hope and realism evident in his voice.

"I will certainly try," I said, projecting more confidence than I felt.

Over the next two days, I worked with Dr. Geller to try to figure out the cause of Mrs. Pool's mysterious weakness. We ordered routine blood tests, and as we analyzed the results, our first clue emerged. A key blood salt known as serum sodium had fallen to a critically low level. We knew that such low salt content could cause excess fluid to flood delicate brain tissues and produce exactly the kind of weakness and lethargy that Mrs. Pool was experiencing. Unless we could identify the cause of the drop in sodium, however, we also knew Mrs. Pool would not be able to recover.

Dr. Geller sent me down three floors to the hospital's medical library to research Mrs. Pool's condition. With a stack of journals piled high in front of me, I pictured Mr. Pool's face — the mixture of sadness, forbearance, and undisguised pain. I wanted so badly to help him, to help both of them, but the odds were stacked against me and Dr. Geller.

After hours of paging through the journals, I found myself examining a study on small cell carcinoma, the type of lung cancer with which Mrs. Pool had been diagnosed. Suddenly, I sat up straight. The small cell tumor, I read, was distinctive in its ability to secrete a potentially deadly substance where it exists in excess called antidiuretic hormone. In healthy people, that hormone was secreted in very small amounts by the pituitary gland, I knew. But in some cancer patients, the article read, this hormone could be released in toxic quantities by the tumor itself, wreaking havoc on the body's ability to regulate salt and water.

The treatment, according to this study, was simple and effective — restrict water intake, which would cause the sodium to rise back to normal levels.

Quickly, I photocopied the pages in the journal and ran back upstairs to find Dr. Geller. He scanned the article, nodding his head several times as he read. Then he looked at me and smiled.

"Let's get started," he said.

25

February 1967

Together, we went to Mrs. Pool's room to detail the course of treatment to her husband. As we explained that while it sounded extreme, she would still be able to have the equivalent of three glasses of water a day — plenty enough to prevent thirst — I watched the expression on his face turn hopeful.

"We think this is a very promising approach," Dr. Geller told him. "But of course, we can't guarantee that it will reverse Mrs. Pool's symptoms."

I found myself anxious, but also hopeful. It had to work!

Later that evening, I went to check on Mrs. Pool and found her husband sleeping on a recliner next to her bed. He probably couldn't afford a hotel room, I thought. Though he'd never mentioned what he did for a living, I'd gathered by his appearance and residence that he was a laborer of some sort, perhaps a farmer.

The next morning at breakfast, I told Eva what I had seen.

"Invite him for dinner," she said immediately. "He probably hasn't had a decent meal or sat in a comfortable chair in a week."

I nodded. I knew it wasn't best practice to fraternize with a patient's family outside of the hospital, but I didn't think there was an actual rule against it.

"Bring him here tonight," she said firmly.

So that evening, I brought Leonard Pool back to our small apartment in Stuyvesant Town. The aroma of roasted chicken was palpable as we walked through the door, and I could see Mr. Pool visibly relax.

"Well now," he said, after I'd made introductions. "This is just what the doctor ordered!"

As the three of us sat around our Formica-topped kitchen table — Adam asleep in the next room — Leonard, as he asked us to call him, told us about Dorothy, an accomplished painter and pianist who lived every day to the fullest and had the best laugh in the world. He and his wife had never had children — the reason for which he did not mention.

Mrs. Pool was responding, ever so slowly, to treatment — her blood pressure had risen slightly and she was now able to speak a few sentences at a time — but I swallowed the urge to reassure her husband with any false hope.

Leonard was easy to open up to, and I found myself telling him about my father and the wave of grief that still overtook me at least once a day. We talked about Adam and the challenges we faced, particularly with another child due in a few short months.

"What field of medicine are you interested in?" he asked me. "Where are you hoping to settle?" He seemed genuinely interested in both of us.

When I asked what he did, he just murmured "this and that" and changed the subject. As the evening came to an end, he said that he hoped when his wife recovered her energy, we would come to visit them in Allentown.

"Allen who?" Eva responded. We all laughed as she admitted she had never heard of Leonard's home town. I didn't add that I hadn't either.

When I returned to the hospital the next morning, I checked in on Mrs. Pool and found her sitting up in bed eating breakfast. Leonard, sitting next to her, was positively beaming.

By the following day, Mrs. Pool was up and moving around the room, chatting with the doctors and nurses who dropped in.

When she was discharged a few days later, both of them hugged me, and I found myself thinking how much I would miss them.

A few weeks later, I was making my rounds when I heard over the loudspeaker, "Dr. Lawrence Levitt. Please report to Mr. Van der Walker's office immediately." My heart froze. Mr. Van der Walker was the president of Memorial Sloan Kettering. This could only be bad news. In the few cases I knew of, this kind of summons had been followed by suspension or even discharge from the program.

As I buzzed the elevator to take me to the top floor, I racked my brain for what I might have done wrong. I hadn't made any major medical errors, as far as I knew. Could I be getting called to the carpet for inviting Leonard to dinner?

When I entered the corner office, I found Mr. Van der Walker sitting behind a massive mahogany desk, with silk drapes lining the windows and a Persian rug sweeping the floor. He was a tall, wiry man, impeccably dressed in a navy three-piece suit, a red tie, and a crisp white shirt. His pale blue eyes were cold.

"Are you Dr. Levitt?" he demanded.

"Yes, Sir," I mumbled.

"Do you remember the Pool case?" he asked in a tone that sounded to me like a bark.

"Of course," I responded, my heart sinking.

"Well, your patient's husband, Leonard Pool, just came to see me," Mr. Van der Walker said. Confused, I watched the corners of his mouth turn up ever so slightly. "You can stop shaking, everything is okay. He wanted to express his appreciation to you and Dr. Geller for the kindness and care you extended to him and his wife."

I could feel myself exhaling in relief.

"Thank you for letting me know, Sir," I replied.

But Mr. Van der Walker wasn't finished. "You may not be aware," he said, "that Leonard Pool is the founder and CEO of a major chemical company, Air Products and Chemicals, in Allentown, Pennsylvania."

My mouth fell open. "Mr. Pool?" I asked incredulously.

"Yes, and in appreciation of your care, he's just pledged one million dollars to Memorial Sloan Kettering."

I stared at him, trying to take in what he had just said.

"So I, in turn, would like to express my thanks to you," said Mr. Van der Walker, standing and walking around to the front of the desk to shake my hand.

I was incredulous as I left his office, and when I told Eva about it, she was simply stunned. The man who had come over to eat her roast chicken, carrots, and potatoes had the means to make that kind of donation?

Leonard never mentioned his gift to me, but he did stay in touch. Mrs. Pool had been able to dine out with friends, paint watercolors, and even play bridge since returning home, he reported. Then, after a couple of months, he called the hospital to say that Dorothy had taken a turn. Would someone be willing to come examine her?

Dr. Geller was too busy to go, so a private plane picked me and a very pregnant Eva up from Teterboro Airport for the quick trip to

Allentown. It may as well have been a foreign country for all we knew of the place.

We dined at Lehigh Country Club, and Leonard showed me the horse stables on his expansive property where Dorothy loved to ride. I spent some time examining Mrs. Pool, but with the advanced stage of her cancer, I couldn't be sure what the problem was. "I suggest you bring her back to the hospital for more tests," I told him.

They did arrive at the hospital a few days later and, unfortunately, the cancer had advanced and there was no further treatment that could help her. They spent a week together there, Leonard sleeping on the recliner next to her each night. She died in the hospital, with her husband by her side.

And as Leonard grieved for his wife and I grieved for my father, our relationship continued to grow.

26

June 1967

At nearly sixteen months, Adam was still nowhere close to walking or talking. "Why us?" we often asked ourselves.

With a new baby on the way, we were not willing to take any chances this time. Eva had found a new obstetrician, a Dr. Birnbaum, affiliated with Cornell but working at Brookdale Hospital in Brooklyn, who patiently fielded our worried questions. I had taken the day off for her scheduled induction, and Eva's parents had agreed to watch Adam. I knew they would be waiting anxiously by the phone for the news.

I thought about the last time we had put them in this position — the initial phone call they had received from the hospital that newborn Adam was having convulsions resulting in likely brain injury, and that he wasn't going to make it. The second phone call an hour later that he had in fact survived. I shuddered at what that must have done to them, and I knew how the thought of it devastated Eva.

We would be checking into the hospital that evening, June 5, 1967, and so we packed our bags and headed to Queens to drop Adam off. We expected an anxious greeting at the door, but when we turned the key and entered the foyer, the only sound we could hear was the blasting of the radio. Upon further inspection, we found Eva's parents huddled around the device in the middle of the dining room table, her grandmother behind the closed door of her bedroom, curled up in worry.

"We've gone to war with Egypt!" her mother hurriedly explained, her attention shifting back to the radio.

We immediately knew the "we" she was referring to was Israel, catching snippets of the broadcast now, Adam squirming in my arms.

In all the excitement of the last few days, I had somehow missed this turn of events, but now I could feel the worry rising in my chest as well, nearly overtaking the fear I felt for my own family. Israel was the safe-haven that ensured that the devastation of the Holocaust could never happen again. Right?

But alas, we needed to be at the hospital. This baby was coming into the world. Now the overwhelming question in my mind had become, what kind of world would welcome this baby?

We handed Adam over, borrowed a portable radio, and said our goodbyes. I would like to say I was fully present during those hours at Brookdale Hospital, but as Eva fought through her contractions, I remained glued to the radio and my mind wandered elsewhere.

By the next day, Israel appeared to be making headway on the battlefront and our son was born — a perfectly healthy baby boy who we named Marc, or Moshe in Hebrew, after my father.

Before Marc's bris — or ritual circumcision — even took place eight days later, Israel had emerged victorious in what came to be known as the Six-Day War. Israel had seized the Gaza Strip, the Sinai Peninsula, the West Bank of the Jordan River, and the Golan Heights.

While the war in Israel felt far away, another distant war, in many ways, hit closer to home. I had watched as friends were drafted to fight in Vietnam, but my years spent preparing to be a doctor had spared me that fate. Under the Berry Plan, physicians were allowed to defer their obligatory military service until they completed medical school and residency training.

With my first year of residency wrapping up and Marc only a few weeks old, I could have been drafted then. Instead, thanks to a letter written on my behalf by Dr. Lawrence Scherr, program director, and Dr. Rulon Rawson, chief of medicine at Memorial Sloan Kettering, I wound up in the U.S. Public Health Service.

The assignment I was given was at the National Communicable Disease Center headquartered in Atlanta, but my tour would be in Tampa, Florida. Having never lived outside of New York, this was a big change. At the time, Tampa was a culturally underdeveloped area and didn't have the offerings or medical care to which we had become accustomed. It did, however, have a big air force base, MacDill, where Eva was allowed to shop at the commissary at a discount.

I worked for the Encephalitis Research Center, a division of the Florida Department of Health, and was expected to investigate epidemics if they occurred. When five hundred students at the University of South Florida fell sick to their stomachs over the winter in 1969, I was sent to find the cause. That research led to what became known as "winter vomiting disease" thanks to a paper I co-authored with that title.

Periodically, I was sent along with other public health officers to Puerto Rico to administer vaccines to schoolchildren. Without fail, each time we walked into a classroom in our white coats, the students would start to cry, knowing what was to come. I learned exactly one sentence of Spanish on those assignments — *el que jora va primero* — he who cries, goes first. A hush would fall over the room at that announcement, and the children would line up and boom, boom, boom, we were out the door.

My interest in neurology was also increasing, both by what I saw professionally and what I was witnessing at home. At that time, the number one cause of acquired intellectual disabilities in children was measles, with one in a thousand measles patients developing measles encephalitis or brain inflammation, with almost certain brain injury. Over one weekend, I assisted in administering twenty eight thousand shots of a new measles vaccine being tested, at one dollar per shot. That effort helped lead to the near elimination of measles from the whole Tampa Bay area and was emulated around the United States.

In my limited free time, I had taken to fishing with Dr. Harry Oard, one of the founders of the American Board of Internal Medicine. Meanwhile, Eva was substitute teaching and taking care of two very young kids. On the days she was working, an older neighbor was called in to babysit for seventy-five cents an hour, the going rate at that time.

Despite our best efforts, it wasn't exactly easy to make friends. Our neighbors had a little girl about Marc's age, and Eva would sometimes take walks with the wife and baby, pushing their carriages down Bon Vivant Drive.

One day, the wife called Eva and asked her for a favor.

"Can you not come by on the weekends?" the neighbor asked. "My husband really doesn't like Jews."

Marc started walking before Adam. Increasingly concerned, we brought Adam to be evaluated by a pediatric neurologist in Gainesville, Dr. Melvin Greer, where his suspected diagnosis was confirmed. Specifically, due to the umbilical cord around his neck at birth, Adam had cerebral palsy.

"What can we do?" we asked Dr. Greer. "There must be something we can do."

"Unfortunately, there isn't," Dr. Greer said. "There are no known early interventions for cerebral palsy patients."

Essentially, he told us, albeit sympathetically, sorry, deal with it.

That wasn't so easy. The tantrums started early, and Adam became increasingly frustrated as he was unable to communicate. He would yell out in the supermarket and sprawl out on the floor, frequently causing Eva to rush out in embarrassment.

"It's not a reflection on us, Eva," I would assure her. "It's who Adam is." I didn't want to admit, even to myself, that I was embarrassed, too.

Adam was four and Marc three when my assignment came to an end. To my own surprise, I had grown to like Tampa and would have considered staying. But the Palmetto bugs that would fly across our room at night were driving Eva crazy, and Florida was just too far from her parents. I accepted a three-year neurology residency at the prestigious Peter Bent Brigham Hospital in Boston, part of the Harvard system. We were heading back up north.

27

June 1970

Living in Boston brought us closer to family, but New York still wasn't exactly around the corner. We didn't know anyone in this new city, and I began working like crazy again, leaving Eva on her own to manage two young kids, one with special needs. After a few months of this, I could tell she was struggling, but I wasn't sure how to help her.

It was a friend at the hospital who recommended Eva see a psychiatrist, and she readily embraced the advice.

"I went to see Dr. Frankel today," Eva said on one of my few evenings at home. She had managed to make dinner while getting the kids bathed and ready for bed. The exhaustion was apparent on her face.

"What did he say?" I asked nervously.

"He said it's very normal for me to be so upset and depressed," she continued. "He's not recommending medicine or ongoing treatment."

While I was disappointed in a way to hear that he would not be able to help her further, I hoped his assessment would prove accurate.

"Will you ask your mother to come up and watch the kids for a few days?" I asked hopefully.

"I'll think about it," she said, and while I knew how much her parents loved their grandsons and wanted to help, she probably wouldn't ask.

It wasn't long before Eva was pregnant again, and with the increased challenge and stress I knew she would be facing, it was time for a vacation. My chief resident recommended Cartagena, Colombia, which was apparently beautiful and inexpensive.

Eva left her mother and young cousin Andrea with strict instructions. Adam was attending special schools by that time, and their strong advice was that he become as independent as possible. If Adam fell down while out for a walk, they were not to pick him up. Instead, they should allow him to get up on his own. He was to maintain his schedule as closely as possible.

With plenty of trepidation and nearly as much excitement, we boarded our plane to Colombia on Eastern Airlines, connecting via Miami. But the flight was delayed just slightly, and when we arrived in Miami, we were greeted with disappointing news — we had just missed our connection, and the next flight to Cartagena was in a week's time. This clearly wasn't going to work for us.

"You could always fly to Barranquilla instead and take a cab to Cartagena," the airline worker suggested. "There's a flight leaving in four hours."

I looked at Eva and she shrugged her shoulders. "We'll take it," I said.

When we arrived in Barranquilla, the airport was steaming hot, with fans blowing in every direction yet doing little to move the heavy air. We managed to find a cab, and my stomach rumbled as we wound our way through barren back roads.

We had been driving about two hours when the car came to a halt. A row of cows was slowly moving its way across the street, so we sat there waiting. Then suddenly, our car was surrounded by eight paramilitary men with rifles pointed straight at us.

"Get out of the car! Put your hands up!" they shouted at us in both English and Spanish.

My mind quickly flashed to the stories I had heard from my in-laws. Being stopped on the Hungarian border. Being taken prisoner on a whim. One glance at Eva, and I could tell she was thinking the same.

Eva was shaking, one arm wrapped protectively around her swollen belly, the other hand digging into my thigh. Were they stopping us because we were Jewish? Would we make it home to our sons?

We did as we were told, raising our fingertips to the back of our heads and slowly exiting the vehicle. We stood helpless as the men patted us down, then demanded the driver open the trunk so they could rifle through our luggage.

After what felt like hours in the sweltering heat, the men yelling to each other in indecipherable Spanish, they tossed our suitcases aside, gave us a nod, and walked away.

Eva and I continued to stand there, stunned. What had just happened?

As if the driver could read our thoughts, he told us in broken English, "They looking for drugs." He seemed rather unphased by the whole encounter.

Still shaking, we repacked our luggage and settled again into the backseat. There were still two hours to go. We managed to have a relaxing visit to Cartagena, and we left plenty of extra time for travel on the return trip.

I hoped the week away had done Eva some good, and upon coming home, I could tell she was settling into life in Boston. Adam was doing fairly well in his special school, and we were encouraged by his slow but real progress in language and ability to care for himself.

Eva found herself a group of moms with kids around Marc's age, and they hit it off. The moms formed a playgroup and would take turns watching the kids, and Eva was able to breathe a little easier on the days she wasn't in charge.

Many nights, I found her sitting in a kitchen chair, the phone cord stretched to the table, deep in conversation with her new friend Avril, one of the other moms.

Avril, I knew, was offering her something that I couldn't; her support was slowly but surely helping to pull Eva out of the fog of young, nearly-single motherhood. I was grateful.

When our daughter Lora was born a few months later at Beth Israel Hospital in Boston, Eva's mother had come up to watch the boys, and Avril called her to see if she could pick up Marc for playgroup. Eva never would have asked her, of course, but she knew it was a great offer, and neither of us ever forgot it.

While life in Boston became more comfortable, I could tell Eva still missed her family desperately, particularly her grandmother Anna. While Anna had survived the ordeal with Brill's disease, she had started to have memory issues, and it was not easy for her to travel. We returned to New York as often as possible to visit.

One Passover, Leonard Pool asked if he might join us for the seder meal in Queens. We had kept in touch regularly through my years in Tampa and now our time in Boston.

A few weeks before his arrival, I received a call from his secretary, Dorothy Hoffner, asking, "What can Leonard read in advance so he will be familiar with the holiday?"

Leonard indeed came well prepared, and after the Four Questions were asked, Leonard pressed me with even more. "Will you stick with neurology?" "Where will you settle?"

I liked neurology as it continuously exposed me to other fields. As a neurologist, you get to see the effect the heart might have on the brain. A woman with breast cancer might have it spread to adjacent nerves in the brachial plexus. A patient may present with metabolic problems like low sodium or an infectious disease like meningitis.

As for where we would settle, that was more up in the air. Staying in Boston was an option — I was enjoying my time at the Brigham, and we were making friends and building a life. I could also easily see our family back in New York, the kids having sleepovers with their grandparents, Eva teaching, me working at one of the many prestigious area hospitals.

But Leonard had his own thoughts on the matter to insert. "How about Allentown?"

28

April 1972

"We couldn't possibly live in Allentown," I told Leonard, deep into the seder's fourth glass of wine. "We need to be in a bigger city."

"Come on, there isn't one neurologist in the whole area. You would be the first," he petitioned. "Just consider it. Think about how many people you could help. Come visit."

So upon returning to Boston, we did just that. Eva's mother and cousin came back to watch the kids, and Leonard sent a private plane to take us to the beautiful Lehigh Valley.

Leonard shuttled us around town in his big black limo. We had lunch at the prestigious Lehigh Country Club once again, visited Hess's department store complete with its afternoon fashion show, and toured the local Jewish Day School. Eva was delighted to see a familiar face teaching there, Carole Langsam, whose parents lived next to her parents in Queens. "What a small world!" they exclaimed upon meeting.

At the end of the busy day, exhausted, we sat down with Leonard to debrief.

"Does Allentown have what you're looking for? Or are we too small-town?" Leonard asked.

"I actually really like the country feel," I told Leonard, dodging Eva's skeptical glances. "Particularly the horses. You know how I love to ride."

"They do have three synagogues, and the Jewish Day School seems really great," Eva mused.

The next day, I met with some of the staff from Allentown Hospital. There were three neurosurgeons, but not one neurologist, only a psychiatrist who would practice neurology when necessary. I was already imagining the impact we could make there.

By the end of the trip, I had accepted a job offer. Before departing, I shook Leonard's hand. "I guess we'll see you soon then."

Two months later, I finished my residency in Boston, and we were on our way to Allentown, Pennsylvania.

We moved into a small flat at The Lakes, an apartment complex off of Cedar Crest Boulevard. I got straight to work building my practice in a small office at 1033 Hamilton Street, the main thoroughfare in center city. I noted how little traffic there was as I commuted between home, the office, and the hospital. What an improved quality of life we would have.

Meanwhile, Eva settled us in at home. We enrolled Marc in kindergarten at the Jewish Day School, and Adam went into the first grade in a Montessori school where there would be more special services available. We joined Congregation Sons of Israel, the modern orthodox synagogue that was within walking distance, and began to build our new life.

Leonard would come by the apartment every day at about 5:00 p.m. I knew this because, on most occasions, I would receive a call from Eva only minutes later and hear her whisper into the phone, "Larry, please come home."

I would arrive to find Leonard, with his Chivas Regal on the rocks, which Eva learned was his favorite, watching Mr. Rogers with the kids.

Other times, he would invite me to ride a horse on his hundred-acre property, and then we would just walk and talk. I was working long, hard hours by this point, and this time together gave us both the chance we needed to unwind.

Then, about three and a half years after we moved to Allentown, came a phone call that changed everything. It was Leonard's second wife, Gloria, on the line. "Larry? You need to come to the house. Now."

I rushed out of the apartment, arriving at nearly the same time as Ed Donley, a close friend and mentee of Leonard's who had taken over the position of CEO at Leonard's company.

We ran inside to find Gloria very upset. Leonard Pool had died in his sleep.

It was later decided to likely be a heart attack that caused his death at the age of sixty-nine. Much like my father nine years prior.

I soon found out that Leonard had left one million dollars to Gloria and fifteen million dollars in his first wife's name to establish the Dorothy Rider Pool Health Care Trust.

I knew that Leonard had been fascinated by the world of medicine from the time he was a boy after watching his sister, Hazel, die from influenza during the 1918 pandemic and seeing his father's mini-strokes from high blood pressure. He had wanted to become a doctor, but financial problems made that impossible.

Instead of going to college, he had to work to support the family after his father died. He saved up the money he made from fixing locomotives in an Erie railroad shop to send his brother Walter to medical school in his stead, and later turned his inventions for safe storage and transportation of unstable gasses into a multimillion-dollar company.

While he deemed it too late for medical school for himself by then, he clearly had found a way to make his mark. I read in the paper that I was to be a Pool Trustee, filling the "doctor" position as he had established it. Ed Donley filled the "businessman" role, Leonard's lawyer, Bob Conrad, the "lawyer" position, and the three of us were charged with naming the fourth trustee in the "other" category.

The mission of the Trust was to serve as a resource that enabled the Allentown and Sacred Heart Hospital Center — later renamed Lehigh Valley Hospital after Sacred Heart pulled out of the merged venture — to be a superior regional hospital and improve the health of the citizens of the region it serves.

And as I continued to grow my own footprint in the region, I knew I now had the opportunity to make a difference on a much grander scale.

29

March 1976

As the Pool Trust took off, so did my practice.

I began recruiting other doctors to join me. Peter Barbour, a Stanford graduate, came first, easing the burden so I didn't feel like I had to be on 24/7.

Then one day, I got a call from Alex Reeves, who had helped me at Cornell Medical School.

"The smartest resident we've ever had is looking for a job," Alex told me. "His name is John Castaldo."

I invited John, a graduate of Dartmouth, to come to Allentown for an interview, wisely asking him to spend the night at our house first. What he didn't know was that the real interview was with Eva. As we walked out the door the next morning, I turned to give Eva a last glance, and she gave me a quick thumbs up.

When Alex Ray Grant joined us from the University of Western Ontario, we moved out to the Cedar Crest campus of Lehigh Valley Hospital. The four of us would consult each other every night on cases over the phone, and gather in a room together once a week to discuss the difficult ones, often with the patient present. We worked on a rotation — two weeks at the office, one at the hospital, and one "other" where we could spend time on writing and research.

At home we had also moved to a bigger house nearby that could accommodate our family. While juggling the kids, their schooling, and volunteering in the Jewish community, Eva took on special training to become an EEG technician so she could help with the practice. Eventually, she moved on from this to become our office manager.

No job was too small or simple for her, including answering the phone and, if necessary, making special arrangements for emergency slots for patients to be seen. She oversaw the office's "acts of kindness," including special personal condolence letters that went to the families of our patients who passed on despite our efforts. The doctors were able to concentrate on the practice of medicine while Eva and her crew handled the rest.

She had a special knack for hiring devoted staff. Our staff would always rise to the occasion, coming in at times of snow or storm when other offices stayed closed. From this group, Eva and I developed close friendships with a half dozen couples and their families, and we shared joyous and trying times.

Both inside and outside of the office, Eva developed a reputation as "the source," giving advice to others about doctors or dentists to go to for care, the best stores to shop at, or which cleaner or seamstress was the absolute must-use. She had a special talent for removing stains, and she did so for multiple friends and neighbors.

Likewise, Eva was known to respond to special needs as she saw them. I was often dispatched to deliver soup to those who were recovering from illness, visit those who were confined to their homes, or invite guests to Shabbat dinner.

One Shabbat, she invited Sol, a resident of the Good Shepherd Home for the Chronically Ill, to join us for the weekly ritual meal that marked the beginning of a day of rest. Sol had spastic cerebral palsy, and after securing his arms under the armrests of his wheelchair so he would not knock over the food, she gave our children the opportunity to do a mitzvah — or good deed — and feed him dinner.

She loved to knit and did so for charitable causes, raising thousands of dollars by selling afghans, scarves, and hats, which she created with beautiful colors. Eva attended dozens and dozens of meetings on boards in the community. She would characteristically come with her knitting bag and make use of that time to knit yet another item. A friend, neighbor, or even an acquaintance going through a trying time would often find a hand-knitted Eva Levitt creation on their front porch.

In addition to the unwavering care she offered to family and community, Eva's instincts were nearly unparalleled.

On one occasion, her mother was admitted to Lehigh Valley Hospital for a routine removal of hemorrhoids. After the procedure, she returned to her room complaining of a severe headache and began to vomit. Her surgeon decided to call in gastroenterology, and that doctor pronounced that Olga was suffering a "gastric ulceration" due to nerves.

But Eva didn't buy it. She knew her mother wasn't particularly nervous about the procedure. It had to be something else. When the doctor left, she called me at my office, which was attached to the hospital.

"Come up to my mom's room right away. Something is terribly wrong with her," she said.

When I reached the room and examined Olga at Eva's request, I noticed an enlarged pupil in her right eye, on the same side of her face as the headache. I called in her internist, Dr. Joe Candio, and he and I quickly concluded that Eva's mom was actually suffering an acute glaucoma attack caused by scopolamine, an anesthetic she'd been given for the hemorrhoid surgery.

Her ophthalmologist, Dr. Tom Burkholder, was quickly called in and confirmed the tentative diagnosis. He gave her an eyedrop antidote to prevent blindness and performed a surgical procedure that allowed fluid to drain from her eye, thus preventing a recurrence. There was no question: Eva's refusal to automatically bow to the initial diagnosis, paired with her considerable powers of observation and intuition, had saved her mother's eyesight.

On another occasion, when Marc was about twelve, he and I were preparing to go on a Memorial Day weekend father-son fishing trip on a remote island in Canada. The plan was that my friend Milton, who had his own private plane, would fly us and two of his buddies to Montreal. From there, the five of us would board a seaplane that would deliver us to a tiny island that could only be reached by air or boat.

The trip itself would be an adventure, and we couldn't wait to get our lines in the water. In that remote slice of the Gouin Reservoir due north of Montreal, the fishing for pike and walleye was phenomenal.

On the morning we were scheduled to depart, Milton showed up at our house at 7:00 as planned. But Marc reported that he'd been up during the night "not feeling very well." He'd had some stomach pain, which I chalked up to his nervousness and excitement about the trip.

"Don't worry about it," I reassured him as we finished breakfast. "You'll feel better once we get up to Canada and you start catching those fish."

But then I noticed Eva standing in the doorway of the kitchen, her arms crossed tightly across her chest. "He's not going," she said plainly.

"What do you mean he's not going?" I demanded.

"I mean, he's not going," she repeated firmly. "This isn't the usual nervous stomach. I don't know what's wrong, but I have a bad feeling about it."

From the doorway, I heard Milton say jauntily, "Ah, come on, he'll be fine," but Eva wouldn't budge.

Marc knew better than to cross his mother, but the look of disappointment on his face was almost more than I could bear. I hugged him, promised another trip soon, and Milton and I drove by ourselves to the airport.

On the flight up to Montreal, I wondered whether Marc was really sick or if his mother was just being overprotective. If so, I felt bad for my son. He'd been so enthusiastic about this trip that he packed a week in advance.

When we reached Montreal, I called home to check in. No one answered. That's strange, I thought; it was still early in the day, and they should be home.

I then called my mother-in-law, who was in daily touch.

"Do you know where Eva and the kids are?" I asked. There was a tense silence.

"They're in the hospital," she reported. "Eva is waiting for Marc to come out of surgery. He had acute appendicitis."

The phone nearly dropped from my hand. Thank God I had listened to Eva. If I hadn't, if instead I had taken Marc to a remote Canadian island which didn't even have a telephone, I shudder to think what could have happened.

It's also why I'll always be grateful that, on so many occasions, we followed her instincts when it came to Adam.

30

February 1979

During the early part of Adam's childhood, we were encouraged by his slow but real progress in language and ability to care for himself. But by age ten, he'd reached a plateau. He could take care of his personal needs, eat by himself, dress himself, go to the bathroom and walk with only very mild left-sided weakness. However, he continued to speak in only the briefest sentences, read at an elementary level, and remained unable to do simple math. Improvement ceased. We began to realize that our son would need special care for the rest of his life. Regardless of what we tried to do for him, Adam would never be fully independent.

It was hard to tell this from the outside. As he grew into adolescence, Adam became tall and handsome, with rusty blond hair and blue eyes. He walked with a slight limp, but otherwise looked like any other pre-teen.

And like other Jewish boys his age, we thought it important that Adam prepare to become a Bar Mitzvah.

For months before the occasion, Adam studied the prayers he would recite. He knew them very well. Finally, the day arrived, and we proudly gathered with more than one hundred people at Congregation Sons of Israel in Allentown.

Eva's parents sat anxiously waiting in the second pew. My mother and sisters and our extended families were there. All eyes were on Adam, who sat with us in the front row, waiting to be called to the *bimah*, the raised platform at the front of the sanctuary.

When the moment came for Adam to walk to the pulpit, he called out hoarsely from his seat, "I'm not going."

A hush came over the room. Mark, a good friend of ours, tried to calm Adam and persuade him to walk up the aisle.

"I'm not going!" Adam repeated in an even louder voice.

Our friends, family, and fellow congregants sat perfectly still. Then our rabbi, Yehuda Pinsky, came off the pulpit and walked over to Adam's pew. The rabbi stood over Adam and said a quiet prayer. Rabbi Pinsky then returned to the pulpit and addressed the congregation, "What Bar Mitzvah is really about is the preparation that takes place, not the words the boy says."

The milestone that occurs as a boy moves from childhood to adolescence had already taken place, he explained. He closed by asking us to remember to treat each other — whatever our needs or abilities — with sensitivity, consideration and respect. There was not a dry eye in the synagogue.

Shortly after Adam's bar mitzvah, Eva's beloved grandmother fell ill. While juggling the three kids and Adam's growing needs and working in the office, we spent as much time as we could driving back and forth to Queens to visit with her. Sadly, her mind had deteriorated over the years prior due to Alzheimer's. She died in 1979 at the age of eighty — fifteen years after her near-fatal episode of Brill's disease.

With Eva's Babi gone, her parents shifted their focus to their only daughter. Could they be more helpful if they were closer?

It would be difficult to leave their family in New York, but Laci and Olga worshiped their daughter and would do anything for her. They were moving to Allentown.

They settled in a modest house about four blocks away from Congregation Sons of Israel, close enough so that they could walk on Saturdays. In the afternoons, they were there to greet the children after school while Eva and I worked.

Eva's father often ran carpool, shuttling our kids to tennis or karate. Her mother made dinner for us every night — often we would pick it up at her place and come home to eat. Everything she made — stuffed cabbage, brisket, goulash — was the best thing I've ever eaten. With Eva working at the office, Olga was the presence in the home, greeting the kids after school. On Friday evenings, we always had Shabbat dinner together.

The children were thrilled to have Anu and Apu close by, never realizing they were calling them "mother" and "father" instead of "grandma" and "grandpa" in Hungarian, because that's what Eva called them.

Most helpful for us, Eva's parents were great with Adam. This gave us the opportunity to have a little breathing room in our lives, occasionally going out to dinner or to a community event.

When Adam turned fourteen, a friend suggested that it might be a good idea to send him to summer camp. Initially, we resisted the idea. "How would the other children react to him?" we wondered. "Would he be safe?"

Then we learned about a camp in Springfield, Massachusetts, called Camp Ramah, which included four hundred and fifty able-bodied children and a program called Tikvah (meaning "hope" in Hebrew), made up of fifty teens and young adults with special needs. We'd heard that the able-bodied kids were particularly kind to the special-needs children and included them in a variety of activities, including swimming, dancing, hiking, and arts and crafts. We became hopeful. We signed Adam up.

Nonetheless, driving up to the camp and dropping Adam off, we worried, would he *really* be okay? Would the other campers really treat him well?

We felt much better once we arrived and the Tikvah program director, Herb Greenberg, walked up to us and put his arm around Adam.

"Don't worry," he told us gently. "We'll take good care of him."

Much to our surprise, Adam waved to us and said, "Bye, bye, Mom and Dad." Then he began to walk up the hill with Herb.

On visiting day, we went back up to the camp and watched Adam perform in a play with the other campers. He sang in the chorus and wore a big smile. The camp indeed was a wonderful place. Everyone ate together and participated in Friday night services. Everyone seemed to love Adam, greeting him as he walked by with his infectious smile.

Everyone went on outings together, and the Tikvah campers even joined the others in "color war," in which the whole camp is split into two teams, and the teams compete against each other in various activities, especially athletics.

Toward the end of Adam's camp experience, Herb suggested that we begin thinking about a permanent placement for Adam once he reached early adulthood. He reminded Eva and me that we would not be around forever, and that Adam might be better off with people of his own abilities rather than staying home with us, isolated from his peers.

We thought about this very seriously. Our son needed to develop as much independence as he could. At the same time, we continued to feel the urge to protect him. The question nagged, could he really be safe and happy without us?

Upon returning home, we consulted with two other families we knew in similar situations. I had met Norman Sarachek, a cardiologist, through my work at the hospital, and knew that he had comparable concerns for his daughter Becky. I was familiar with David Bergstein, his wife Clara, and their daughter Ally through the Jewish community.

We knew there were facilities out there, but none in our area that would specifically cater to members of the Jewish community and their needs, kosher food among them. So together, we began the process of establishing our own group home.

Our first step was to meet with David Austin, president of LifePath, a provider of services to group homes. For some reason, he took a liking to us.

After hearing our stories, and despite the hurdles we knew we would face, David said, "I'll help you do this."

David guided us to establish ourselves as an official nonprofit, which we called Tikvah House, a nod to the program at Ramah that had sparked this journey. We formed a board of directors made up of twelve community members, with four seats turning over each year. I became the board's first president.

We had a long way to go, but it brought us great comfort to know that we were preparing for Adam's future.

31

June 1982

With Adam off to Camp Ramah for the summer, my father-in-law came to me one day and said, "Larry, I think it's time we take a trip."

With their grandparents in town, Marc and Lora had become increasingly curious about their life during the war. Going back to Czechoslovakia was something I knew Laci had wanted to do for many years. He wanted to show his family where he was born, what he had endured, and how he had managed to survive.

Eva was initially reluctant to see evidence of the horrors she had been told about. "What good can come of this?" she asked me. I honestly wasn't sure. Finally, for her father's sake, Eva agreed to go.

We did our best to prepare ourselves for the grief and rage we would surely feel in this encounter with memories of unspeakable cruelty. What we didn't expect were our encounters with other realms of the human heart — ones that mystified, humbled, and, finally, helped to heal us.

So we packed our bags and flew with fifteen-year-old Marc and twelve-year-old Lora to France, where we boarded a train bound for Humenné.

Czechoslovakia was still under Communist control at the time, and as soon as we crossed the border, guards began walking up and down the aisles of the train. They stopped at our cabin, and Lora looked on, frightened, as the guards pulled her luggage off the top rack and began rummaging through it. When they found nothing of interest, they shoved everything back in her suitcase and hastily moved on.

After a long and tiring journey, we arrived in the small town of Humenné, the town where Olga was raised, where Eva was born, where they lived as a family with Olga's parents, under the shadow of war yet happy to be together. Olga was immediately stricken, pointing out where the butcher shop, the flower shop, and the town center once stood. Laci noted the police station where he had frequent encounters.

We made our way through town until we reached a modest house attached to what was once a vinegar factory. We spotted an enormous garden in the back of the house and a lovely courtyard in the front.

The mixed emotions were evident on Laci and Olga's faces. This home represented the life they could have had. From the stories they told, I could almost picture Morris Roth closing up the vinegar factory after a long day's work, wiping his boots before coming in for dinner, and kissing his wife Anna in greeting.

I watched Eva carefully; she was not remembering exactly, but piecing together bits of stories she had been told.

We stood there for a while as Laci told his grandchildren about the events that had taken place in this house — a moment of healing for him, and one of realization for them.

"Now, kids, let me show you where I was born," he told Marc and Lora.

We traveled the twenty-five miles to Radvan, where Laci and his brother Jack had taken over their father's lumber business, a business they were ultimately forced to abandon.

As we approached the small village on that sunlit afternoon, we were struck by the sight of dozens of people running through town clasping bouquets of yellow daisies. We couldn't make out what they were saying at first, but then we heard it: "Ritter! Ritter!" Evidently, the villagers had caught wind that the now seventy-five-year-old Leopold Ritter, their former employer, was returning to his hometown after a thirty-four-year absence.

We knew Laci had been a respected business owner, but we were overcome with this reception. The villagers told us what a kind and generous boss Laci had been, often lending money to workers in need and going out of his way to help others.

We walked the town's narrow roads. The village was dotted with small, thatched-roof houses made of wood or stone, many of them brightened by phlox and daisies in the front yards and vegetable gardens in the back. We stopped at a stand on the edge of the road and bought fresh tomatoes, beans, apples, and potatoes, sold to us by round-faced women in babushkas. "It's almost as I remembered it," Laci said softly.

Then, spotting an elderly man walking stiffly toward him, Laci cried out. The two men haltingly made their way toward each other, laughing and shouting. They wrapped each other in a long bear hug and then spoke quickly to each other in Slovak. Finally, Laci brought the man over to us.

"This is Jozef," he told us, his arm draped around the old man's thin shoulder. He told us that when all exemptions for Jews were canceled, Jozef had tried to save his father Moshe, who had leg trouble, by carrying him up the mountain on his back, with Laci's mother Eugenia walking alongside.

Each of us, in turn, clasped Jozef's outstretched hand. I thought of the old saying, "He's not heavy, he's my brother." But I'd never known anyone who had literally enacted that saying, risking his own life to try to carry another to safety. Would I have done the same?

After a number of hours, we said our goodbyes and returned to our hotel for the night. We knew the day ahead would be rough, and getting a good night's sleep was paramount.

Early the next morning, two drivers picked us up at our hotel and we headed north to Poland. When we reached the border, however, one of our drivers was found to have some irregularity with his license and was not able to continue.

At that point, hours into the trip already, we had little choice — seven of us crammed into one compact car, and we continued our journey. Eva crouched on the floor of the passenger seat in front of her father while the rest of us bunched ourselves in the back.

The four-hour trip was hot and dusty with no air conditioning. We found ourselves uncharacteristically quiet, not daring to complain about the conditions, unsure of what we would find or how we would feel when we finally arrived at Auschwitz.

As we passed through the iron gates at the entrance to Auschwitz, the first thing we saw was the heinous, duplicitous sign at the top: "Arbeit Macht Frei" ("Labor Brings Freedom"). As we approached the gas chambers, Laci, his voice shaking, told us how his parents had been ordered on arrival to "go to the showers," the selection made by the infamous Nazi doctor Josef Mengele.

The "showers," of course, were actually Nazi euphemisms for gas chambers, ready for prisoners who appeared too old or weak to work. We knew 1.5 million people in all were murdered in those chambers.

There were no signs explaining what we were seeing; we relied on Laci to tell us what he had seen and experienced with his own eyes. For Olga, whose mother had also endured these horrors, her first visit to the site left her nearly unable to speak past the lump in her throat.

Laci took us to the crematoria where the gassed bodies were taken to be burned. He pointed out the tall smokestacks. "How could the people in the town of Auschwitz, across the street, deny that they knew what was going on?" he asked, his voice low and tight. "They knew."

For all of us, the crematoria were the most painful to absorb. Made of stone and brown brick, the structures were fitted with metal doors and sliding mechanisms that allowed the bodies to be pushed in and, later, the ashes to be removed.

When Eva saw some ashes around the crematoria, she recoiled. "Could these be...?" she whispered to me. I found myself unable to speak. Hearing about the horrors of Auschwitz had been one thing. But actually seeing the killing machines was something else entirely, an electric shock to the body, mind, and soul. Eva's hand gripped mine.

For our children, I know, this was especially haunting. They had learned about the Holocaust in school, heard stories from their own grandparents, were familiar with their Apu's tattooed forearm number, yet to see it with their own eyes I believe solidified their resolve to make sure something like this could never happen again.

We went across the road to Birkenau, where Laci showed us the actual bunk where he slept with five other prisoners. I stared at the rough wooden structure, which measured about three feet high, six feet deep, and twelve feet across, forcing the six prisoners to lie sideways in order to fit. I tried to imagine myself struggling to survive such extremes of confinement. How did Laci survive?

When I asked him, he was quiet for a moment. Then he said, "I never stopped thinking of Olga and Eva, and I kept my faith."

"Your father survived here, in this horrible place," Eva's mother said to her as we prepared to depart. "Now, I want to show you why you and I are here today, why your children are here."

Eva knew well, of course, of the Catholic couple who had kept them hidden during the war while her father and grandparents were gone, their fates unknown. She had heard the stories, her mother had translated their letters, and Eva even sent over her wedding dress for one of their daughters to wear. But she was a young girl the last time she saw them. Essentially, they had never met.

Deeply shaken, we left Auschwitz for the long, quiet ride to Bratislava.

32

July 1982

When we arrived at the Hajtas' small cement house, we walked through a black metal gate into a garden dancing with orange, yellow, and pale pink daylilies. A small backyard had been dug up into a vegetable and fruit garden, with fat tomatoes hanging off their stems and pea and bean plants snaking their way up trellises.

Though Geza had found success working for the railroad during and after the war, economic conditions under Communist rule had led to struggles. I knew my father-in-law had sent over enough money for the Hajtases to purchase an extra parcel of land to set up their garden and grow their own food.

At the door, we were welcomed by the Hajtases with hugs and much delight. We were all excited to meet their daughter Katka, born after the war. Geza was a bald-headed, bright-eyed man of sixty-nine by then with an enormous belly and a laugh to match. His wife Klara, sixty-five, tall and majestic, guided us into their living room, where I noticed several statues of Jesus and Mary and crucifixes adorning the walls.

"Evitchka!" Klara said, embracing Eva, who must have been almost unrecognizable to them as a woman in her forties.

Olga and Laci talked a mile a minute with Geza and Klara, catching up as old friends do. The problem was, the entire conversation was in Slovak, which I couldn't understand. Eva was able to communicate in Hungarian, and I relied on their translations to take part. We learned that the Hajtases remained devout Roman Catholics throughout all they had seen. We came to find out that Olga, Eva, and Munci were not the only Jews they had helped during the war; in fact, they had saved more than a dozen with Geza using his position at the railroad to make use of service coaches, inspection rooms, and uniforms.

For dinner that night, Klara proudly served kosher chicken that she had gone all the way across town to procure. As the platters were served, I watched Laci eye it carefully, and I knew what he was thinking — though the product was kosher, it wasn't cooked in a kosher kitchen, negating its value.

"Eat it anyway," I mouthed to him across the table. And he did.

The Hajtases graciously hosted our whole family in their home, and before we left the next morning, I asked Eva to relay a question to Geza: "Why did you do it?"

He put his arm around me and said in Slovak, "Young man, a good life comes from working hard and helping other people."

We kept in regular touch with the Hajtases after that through letters and phone calls. Knowing what they had done for my wife's family, for our family, I felt compelled to help them in any way I could, and I know Eva felt the same. But how often do you get the chance to do something truly meaningful for someone who risked his life to save yours? As fate would have it, that opportunity came about five years later.

We learned that Geza had begun to suffer serious health problems. The doctors in Bratislava had told him that he had an enlarged prostate, but they advised that he was "too old, too heavy, and too fragile" to undergo the necessary operation, called a transurethral prostatectomy. I worried that if Geza's symptoms worsened, he would encounter still more debilitating and painful medical problems. I also knew that the Hajtases had limited funds for medical care outside their own country.

I spoke with several doctors and administrative officials in my network at Lehigh Valley Hospital. When I told each person Geza's story, the response was immediate: "We will be happy to treat him without charge." Eva and I relayed the news to Geza and Klara excitedly, sent them plane tickets, and soon they were arriving at our home in Allentown.

One week later, Geza underwent surgery at Lehigh Valley Hospital. Dr. Stanley Zeeman, senior cardiologist, oversaw his cardiac care. Dr. John Jaffe, a skilled urologist, performed the surgery pro bono. The surgery was a success.

John, also a friend of mine, would later tell me that when Geza first came into his office, he felt moved to thank his patient. "For what?" asked the puzzled Geza in Slovak as Laci acted as translator.

"For your courage in risking your life for others," John responded, surprised to hear himself saying something so personal to a patient. John recalls Geza shrugging and saying, "It was what anyone would do." John certainly knew it wasn't.

Later, during the discharge process, John surprised himself again — he spontaneously hugged his patient goodbye.

The Hajtases stayed with us for three months as Geza recovered from his surgery. He lived another eight years. During that time, Eva and I filled out all the paperwork and submitted for review his and Klara's story, asking the government of Israel to recognize them as

"Righteous Among the Nations," a sacred term given to non-Jews who saved the lives of Jews during the war. A plaque in their honor stands today at Yad Vashem, Israel's Holocaust memorial.

33

October 1987

At the same time as we were figuring out how to help the Hajtases, we were also getting Tikvah House off the ground. We secured support from the state and county, and as Adam got older and prepared to finish school, we knew it was time to purchase a property.

Along with the Sarachek and Bergstein families, we bought a house nearby where Adam, Becky, and Ally could live. Each family was responsible for their child's room, and furnishing the common areas was a group effort.

At age twenty-one, we moved Adam into Tikvah House. He and his roommates got along nicely from the start. Thanks to LifePath, a service provider for disabled adults, it was set up so that an attendant would be on hand at all hours to help the Tikvah House residents. That included providing them with three kosher meals a day and taking them for walks and for outings like to the movies or for ice cream.

In turn, it allowed us to live more of a "normal" life knowing that Adam was well cared for nearby and that he was happy.

With Adam settled, Eva and I started to look back at the impact raising a special-needs child had on our marriage and on our other two children.

The truth is, having a child with needs like Adam's poses an extra strain on one's marriage. In the early years of raising Adam, there was certainly a strain on ours. I found myself less patient than I should have been, and less appreciative of Eva's enormous contribution to the effort of raising our children.

For Marc and Lora, having a brother like Adam meant constantly having to fight for our attention, which manifested in fighting with each other, leaving Eva to constantly referee.

Several couples whom we know well, and who have special-needs children, have divorced. That pattern is unfortunately true nationally. I think we managed to thrive, and maybe even strengthen our marriage, in spite of much pain and stress because we were able to accept Adam's challenges quite early in the process. This is a testament to Eva and her unwavering strength.

That strength was never more apparent than when her mother got sick a few years later. At first, we didn't know what was wrong, and many doctors' appointments and hospital visits brought few answers. Mulling it over on a flight to California with Eva, I had an epiphany — it had to be cancer.

I called a friend at Memorial Sloan Kettering, and he agreed to evaluate her right away. The problem was, we were three thousand miles away.

I arranged for an ambulance to transport her from Allentown to New York, and then called my son Marc, who had just started medical school in the Bronx at the Albert Einstein College of Medicine.

"I need you to drive to Allentown, organize her transfer, and then ride with her in the ambulance," I told him.

Having endured the early days of medical school myself, I knew this was a big ask, but I also knew Marc would do anything for his Anu, and so he went.

Late that night, Marc called back. Anu had been examined, tests had been run, and a full team of doctors had gathered in her room to report the diagnosis. The lead physician, he reported, coldly pronounced the news from the hospital room doorway, "You have multiple myeloma and will be starting chemotherapy tomorrow."

The diagnosis and follow-up plan were accurate. The delivery, however, was not exactly setting a good example for my soon-to-be-doctor son. In fact, he told us later, it left him in awe of the medical process, yet taught him exactly what not to do in the care of a patient.

Olga returned to Allentown for treatment, where Eva could drive her to appointments and take care of her needs. She died in our home at the age of seventy-eight, five years after her cancer diagnosis.

34

June 1994

It wasn't too long after Olga's passing that Laci moved into our house. Tired of tending two homes, we built an addition for him, forever known as "Apu's room."

Eva doted on her father, as we all did, wanting to do anything she could to make him happy, but he continuously ribbed her with his sly sense of humor. One weekend, we rented a house in the Poconos and while it was meant to be a time for relaxation, Eva knew how important Shabbat was to Laci. She packed the car full of everything we would need, and when we arrived, she set the table with a nice white table cloth, candlesticks, and wine. After the blessings were said, Laci looked at Eva with a glimmer in his eye and said, "What? No soup?"

Back at home, Laci kept himself busy, swimming at the Jewish Community Center and joining a poker club with friends, who rotated hosting the weekly games. On Saturdays, I accompanied him to synagogue where he served as the "gabbi," responsible for calling everyone up to the *bimah*, or platform, to take their honors of a blessing over the Torah. When he could no longer stand for long periods, they got him a stool. When he could no longer walk to synagogue, I would push him in his wheelchair down Tilghman Street.

He never liked to be late. I would come down in the morning to have my coffee and find him sitting in the entrance to the garage, all dressed up in his suit, gloves, and scarf.

"I'm not leaving until 8:30!" I would tell him repeatedly.

"Did I say anything?" he always replied innocently.

He was a heftier man by that time, and the road was full of dips and divots; I was often sweating profusely by the time we arrived. But we had the best talks on these walks.

We talked about the war, his early days in America, and his years operating a cigar and newsstand in the Drake Hotel.

By the time I met Laci, I could tell he was fed up with the butcher business. He had started working with a new partner in Kew Garden Hills whom he found to be too rough around the edges. "If you continue working there, you'll get ulcers," I told him.

I was an intern at Bellevue at the time and had seen in *The New York Times* an advertisement for a newsstand for sale in the Gotham Hotel. I urged Laci to go check it out, and before I knew it, he had handed over a check.

Olga left her job at the tie factory to join him in the newsstand. They sold sightseeing tickets, theater tickets, and were able to make a living, but it wasn't a big hotel. Every evening they would drive home past the Drake, and at least once a week I heard Laci express how he would like to be there, where it was always busy.

About three and a half years into the gig, a frequent customer approached him. I like how you handle this business, he told him. Would you consider taking over the stand at the Drake?

"When he told me, I thought God sent him," Laci gushed over dinner.

Coincidentally, their lease at the Gotham happened to be up, so they transferred their operation to the Drake and remained there for ten years, able to make a nice living before moving to Allentown.

In the summer of 1997, after Olga and Geza had passed on, Klara Hajtas came to visit. We had continued to keep in regular touch and were delighted to see her. And, it just so happened that her visit coincided with a very special occasion. In celebration of the fiftieth wedding anniversary of Munci and Joseph Goldberg, their sons Mark and Steven and their seven grandchildren would be dedicating a Sefer — or handwritten — Torah in their honor.

We traveled to Queens together with Laci and Klara for the ceremony and party to follow. Munci's son Mark spoke first, noting that he and his brother were raised by the guiding principle of "everything for the children."

"I stand in awe when I think of all the challenges they faced for themselves after suffering the loss of their families and trying to rebuild themselves," he said of his parents. "My aunts and uncles are all a testimony to the strength and resilience of our people and our faith in God. To those who sought to destroy us, our answer is the eternal Torah."

Then Munci, a petite woman in her late seventies, got up to speak.

"I would like to thank everyone for honoring us with your presence at our simcha. We thank Hashem for sparing our lives during the Holocaust. I'm grateful to my two brothers, Laci and Jack, for doing everything possible to save me during that time."

Sitting next to me in his wheelchair, I spied a tear sliding down Laci's cheek. Then, I watched as Munci's eyes turned to the tall, white-haired woman, sitting with us in the back of the room.

"There is another person here today who is responsible for saving me and my family," Eva's Aunt Munci told her friends and family. "Please, will you come up here?"

The crowd was silent as Klara Hajtas made her way to the front of the room. "Klarika," Munci greeted her warmly, and then spoke to her in Slovak, words that I didn't understand, but their meaning was evident. When she finished speaking, the two women embraced, Klara kissing Munci on each cheek.

When the ceremony ended, the family danced and laughed for hours, just happy to be together.

It wasn't long after this that Laci began having pain in his chest. I brought him to Lehigh Valley Hospital, where it was determined that he needed to have open heart surgery. At ninety, he wasn't exactly a prime candidate, but I convinced my friend Dr. Ray Singer, one of the most prominent heart surgeons in Pennsylvania, to do the surgery.

After Ray walked out of the operating room, Eva said to him, "You look terrible."

"I was operating on Larry Levitt's father-in-law, so that was stressful," he told her honestly. "And if Hitler didn't kill him, I didn't want to be the one to do him in."

And he didn't. Laci lived another five years after that, having the opportunity to meet five great-grandchildren and pass away in "Apu's room" in 2002 at the age of ninety-five.

35

December 2002

Laci's passing hit all of us hard, and it was around this time that I realized that the stress of my job was also getting to me.

Our neurology practice had been successful for thirty years. In all that time, we had never been sued once, which I attribute to not only being good at our jobs, but also owning up to our mistakes. I wasn't like Eva or our son Marc who took challenges in stride and used them as motivation to work even harder, qualities that clearly came directly from Eva's mother.

My heart would pound each time my pager would go off with an emergency call. Would I get there in time? Would I make the right diagnosis? In truth, I was ready to slow down. It was time to retire.

Eva, however, didn't seem to know the meaning of slow down. She was more involved than ever serving in the Jewish community, hosting Shabbat dinners, doing favors for friends and, especially, helping to raise our grandchildren.

Our first grandchild and only grandson, Sam, was born to Marc and his wife Shary before I retired and while Marc was undergoing his medical training. Raquel and Jessica soon followed.

Marc and Shary met while on an Israel program they both participated in as students at the University of Pennsylvania. Like me, Marc was a good student, yet he was turned down by several of the top-tier medical schools. Like his mother and grandparents, he didn't let that stop him for a minute, combining the best qualities of his Apu and Anu. Laci's philosophy on life was, "Don't have expectations and you won't be disappointed." But Olga had always said to Marc the same thing she said to me when I told her of my intention to propose to Eva: "If you don't ask, you won't get."

At the Albert Einstein College of Medicine, Marc quickly took an interest in surgery, which was of little surprise to us — growing up, we often found him sitting at the kitchen table, meticulously gluing the pieces of a broken plate or vase back into place, inherently knowing how to do it with little instruction. He was also, however, intrigued by pediatrics after his rotation in that department, and when he found out he could combine his two passions, he embarked on the path to become a pediatric surgeon.

One elective he took in school was for pediatric colorectal surgery. It was not a widely covered specialty, and he soon realized the impact he could make by going down this path. I'm proud to say he is now one of the leading pediatric colorectal surgeons in the world, having written five books and spoken at hundreds of national conferences.

I'm most proud, however, of the mission work that he does around the world, and I spend considerable time bragging about the children's lives he's dramatically bettered. Through the nonprofit he founded, Colorectal Team Overseas, Marc organizes twice yearly trips to developing countries to perform life-changing surgeries and to train local staff.

For years, Eva accompanied Marc on these trips, collecting stuffed animals or medical equipment or whatever items were needed and hauling them to far-flung places like Ghana, Vietnam, and Colombia.

On these visits, while Marc was in surgery, Eva would take the time to really get to know the patients and the staff in the way that only she could. I rarely had the opportunity to join them, but I did accompany Marc and Eva on a trip to Hungary.

Before the surgeries began, Marc invited Eva to address the medical school and hospital staff both in English and Hungarian. Once nervous to speak in front of a crowd, Eva confidently delivered her remarks.

"It is an honor and a privilege to say a few words to this conference in Pecs, Hungary. I am beginning in Hungarian since that was the language of my parents and grandparents," she began.

"Permit me to admire what you are doing here. Our son, Marc, is leading a team that will operate on children and hopefully change their lives. Others are here to learn some of these techniques and use them to help change lives in the countries from which you come. In our culture, it is said that saving one life is like saving the world. You are doing that, and I applaud your efforts."

Her confidence reminded me of watching Sam at his bar mitzvah in Cincinnati about thirteen years prior, wrapped in the tallis that Eva made for him, a silver rectangle from her own father's tallis — one that he acquired in America after the war — sewn in. Sam spoke about his grandparents and their Holocaust story, catching the attention of a friend's father. His father-in-law was from Humenné, he told us afterward. It turned out that he was a friend of Eva's Uncle Jack.

Stories like this abound. On a mission to Israel with our local Jewish Federation, Eva was among the first to arrive at a dinner one night with lone soldiers — young adults who volunteer to serve in the Israeli army though their families live outside of Israel.

Eva could have sat anywhere, but she opted for a table with three soldiers and began a conversation. One of the soldiers was from New York, the most outspoken. She told him she was from Allentown, but he asked further, where was Eva's family from?

"A small place in Slovakia, you wouldn't know it," she said.

"No, really," he probed. "Where are you from?"

"It's near Košice," she told him, never dreaming he would know of her small hometown.

"Košice! Where exactly?" So she told him.

With that, the soldier pulled out his cell phone and immediately called his grandfather in New York.

"I'm sitting next to a woman who's from Humenné and her father did business in Radvan," she heard him tell his grandfather excitedly. Before she knew what was happening, he had handed her the phone.

"Are you Laci Ritter's daughter?" he asked her.

"Yes!" she said in disbelief.

"I did business with your father. He was a wonderful man."

And, of course, there was the meeting of the Evas in Allentown.

We were always told that only six Jewish children from Humenné survived the war, but we never knew anything about these other children until about five years ago, when Eva and Albert Derby moved to Allentown.

In a small Jewish community, the arrival of another Holocaust survivor was big news. Eva and Eva quickly became acquainted through their work with the Jewish Federation's Holocaust Resource Center, going into local schools to share their stories.

My Eva was immediately taken aback by how remarkably similar their stories began.

Eva Derby, it turned out, was born in Humenné in July 1942, six months after Eva Ritter. She and her mother were able to obtain false identification papers, which marked her as a "mischling," a person of mixed Jewish and non-Jewish ancestry. Her mother was also able to obtain a false baptismal certificate from a priest stating that her father was Jewish, but her mother was not. Her father left the two of them to join his parents in Poland in May 1942 and never returned.

In 1944, the Gestapo discovered her and her mother's papers were false, and they were taken to Theresienstadt. When they arrived, the camp was full, and she and her mother were placed in an old people's home near Prague, run by a Hungarian Rabbi who saved women and young children. They were liberated by the Soviet army in 1945.

Her mother immigrated to the United States, leaving her with her aunt and uncle in Europe. When her mother obtained enough money four months later, she brought Eva over. She was four years old.

More than seventy years later, what were the chances that two of these six children would end up in the same small Pennsylvania city?

Though many of our friends have moved to Florida or other warmer places since retiring, we never had any intention of leaving Allentown. Mainly because our daughter and son-in-law are here.

While Marc's work brought him from New York to Cincinnati to Columbus, Ohio, and now Washington, D.C., Lora settled in Allentown after meeting her husband, Sharone.

They met at the Israeli airport, in fact — Lora, who was there for the summer, was waiting to pick up Eva who was coming for a visit when an elderly gentleman tripped and fell into her. She stumbled, about to fall, when a young, handsome Israeli soldier caught her in his arms.

They got to talking and he asked for her number. On a gap year volunteer program between college and graduate school and living in a dorm, however, she had no phone number to give him.

Instead, he wrote down his number and handed it to her. "What do I do?" Lora asked Eva when she finally arrived.

"Call him and make a date for coffee in an outdoor cafe," she told her confidently. And that's exactly what Lora did.

The two continued to build their connection after that, but when her program ended, Lora didn't think she'd ever see him again. She returned to New York and started graduate school at Columbia, studying for her master's degree in special education, but soon found out her new sister-in-law Shary would be bringing a group of students to Israel that December. Did she want to go?

She did, and a friend helped her write a letter to Sharone in Hebrew telling him she was coming and asking if he wanted to see her. He told her to give him a call when she arrived, and he came to meet her in Jerusalem for Shabbat. When the trip was over, she spent a few days with his family and they kept in close touch. He came to the States to visit for Passover, and by August he had moved to the U.S. for good.

Lora was working in New York at the time, but Sharone wasn't a fan, so he came to live with Eva and me in Allentown for six months until they got married and settled nearby. Helping to raise their three girls has been one of the highlights of both of our lives.

Ariel was born first, then came Danielle and Talia. We would watch the kids after school and shuttle them to activities. Every night, Eva would make dinner for the family, like her mother did for us, which Sharone would pick up on his way home.

Lora went to work as a special education teacher in the Allentown schools. It's hard to imagine that growing up with Adam didn't contribute to this career choice. Our collective experience with Adam also helped us become more prepared for the challenges Lora's own daughter would face.

Eva knew from an early age that Danielle had special needs, but her pediatrician didn't agree. Eva persisted, however, noting her delayed milestones. She had seen it before.

Finally, when Danielle was three, the pediatrician realized Eva had been right all along. Danielle was diagnosed with autism.

We were fortunate to be very involved in Danielle's upbringing and bring what we had learned with Adam to the table. Yet so much had changed — there were so many more resources available than there ever were for Adam, and we were grateful.

Over the summers, Danielle attended the same Camp Ramah program that Adam had benefited from. The program is now offered at all eight Ramah camps.

On Friday nights, the whole family still would have dinner together. Eva did the cooking for a time, and then Lora took over.

Adam joins us for dinner every Friday and calls me twice a day. Now a man in his fifties, he's still at Tikvah House. He's able to read simple things and repeats the same question often. "Dr. Levitt!" he proclaims each time he sees me, a big smile on his face. He has twenty-four-hour care, companionship, and, most importantly, he is happy. Lora serves as a co-guardian with Marc, and I know they will continue to look after him when we no longer can.

36

December 2021

On the occasion of Eva's approaching eightieth birthday, our entire family gathered right near Disney World in Florida over winter break. It was the first time we had all been together in over two years because of the Covid-19 pandemic.

We had an opportunity to have some one-on-one time with our six grandchildren, asking each one about their lives. Sam told his "Bubbish" — his nickname for Eva — that he was going back to school to get a master's degree in sports management. Raquel would be going to London for a year through her work with AMEX. Ariel was about to graduate from Drexel University with a degree in chemistry, and Jessica would in a few years be graduating from Ohio State with a degree in computer engineering. Danielle was starting to work at Weis supermarket and taking a course of study at Penn State designed for children with autism to enable them to reach their fullest potential. Talia would be finishing up high school at the Jack M. Barrack Hebrew Academy in Bryn Mawr and soon be off to college.

Sharone did a lot of cooking, and we all would gather in Lora and Sharone's condo for meals. At one of these dinners, Marc asked each person to describe Eva in one word.

Lora said "compassionate," Ariel "dependable," Sam "giving." Raquel came out with "thoughtful," Shary "generous," and Marc "resilient." Talia said she was "sincere," Sharone called her "gorgeous inside and out," I called her "selfless," and Adam called her "Mom."

I was immediately taken back to a visit we paid to Klara Hajtas in Bratislava in 2009, long after Geza had passed. After dinner in her home one evening, we showed her some photos of our travels. One of the photos featured Eva and me, our three children, and our six grandchildren striking a pose at Disney World. Our arms were draped around each other, our faces aglow with joy. Klara studied this photo for a long time. When she looked up, tears were streaming down her cheeks. She looked into our eyes. There was no need to explain. We were crying, too.

Without her and Geza and their heroic efforts, without my mother-in-law's utter resilience and determination to protect her young child, her pretty Evitchka, and my father-in-law's drive to survive and give his family a better life, there would be no pictures.

Epilogue

July 2023

A year and a half after her wonderful eightieth birthday celebration, the beautiful, incomparable Eva (Ritter) Levitt passed away peacefully in her home, surrounded by a family that would not have existed were it not for grit, luck, and determination.

Over three hundred and fifty people attended her funeral in Allentown, Pennsylvania. Another fifty plus people watched the streaming service from all over the world.

Immediately, stories and well wishes began pouring in from the hundreds and hundreds of people whose lives she touched.

"Eva was indeed a force. She made things happen and got things done. She was incredibly interesting and smart and fun. I still have a bright green beaded bracelet she bought for me during a foray into the open market in Ghana. I wear it often and think of her when I do. What a special person, and the legacy she leaves behind is a true testament to the life she led."

"Whenever I hear the expression 'force of nature,' I think of Eva. There was no challenge that was too daunting and no problem that couldn't be solved. Her sheer strength was a gift to all of us who knew her, and for anything in which she was involved, there was a comfort in knowing that Eva was taking care of it."

"Eva was always there to support, through thick and thin. She was always present, making sure things were just so, and the people she loved had what they needed, when they needed it, coordinating and conducting in the background. You'd never see her directing in the foreground, but you knew she was there and if you looked hard enough, you'd recognize her touch and concern. And if you were discerning enough, you might catch a glimpse of her guiding hand setting things where they needed to be."

"Marc, I'll never forget making the realization after you told us all your mom's story of survival — had she not survived, you wouldn't have been born, our colorectal program wouldn't have existed, patients and families' quality of life wouldn't have improved, and we wouldn't have had the dream job/team that we did. It all stemmed back to her. Without her, none of it would have been possible. What an incredible legacy she left you with and everyone she met in her lifetime."

May her memory be a blessing and her incredible legacy live on.

Acknowledgments

From the seedling of an idea, we are so grateful to the many, many people who played a part in *Evitchka*'s publication.

Thank you to Mark Goldberg who shared invaluable resources, including video interviews with his mother Munci and his Uncle Laci.

Those interviews, conducted and cataloged in the 1990s by Steven Spielberg's USC Shoah Foundation, truly brought this story to life in a way that nothing else could.

An oral history interview conducted by Joan Ringelheim with Olga Ritter in 1982 and gifted to the United States Holocaust Memorial Museum Collection similarly enabled us to tell a critical piece of the story from Olga's perspective.

While no recording of Jack Ritter could be located, his daughter Judy Rosen offered her insights.

Thank you to Eva's cousin Andrea Kesar, Lew and Anne Rothman, and Avril Danziger for sharing their own memories.

As we embarked on the writing process, wonderful friends offered their feedback. Thank you to Judy Morrison, Deena Scoblionko, Avril Danziger, Steve Lewis, Margie Clark, Jessica Zolotsky, and the many others who provided encouragement.

Another of those early readers was Ann Wlazelek, who had just published her own children's book and brilliantly suggested we submit our manuscript to Crave Press.

A million thank yous to Christina Steffy and David Reimer for taking a chance on us and this book. Your partnership has meant the world to us.

To Adam Levitt, Marc and Shary Levitt, and Lora and Sharone Vaknin — your support has been absolutely critical and is so appreciated.

Sam, Raquel, Jessica, Ariel, Danielle, and Talia — your Zayde loves you so much.

Adam, Emma, and Lily Smartschan — thank you for allowing your wife/mother the time and space to work on something so meaningful.

And finally, thank you to the one and only, the incomparable Eva Levitt, who was enthusiastic about this book from the get-go and shared her own memories over many months. We found out this book was likely to be published only days after Eva passed. Working on this project has brought joy and comfort to a sad time. We feel incredibly fortunate to be able to share this true story with the world.

About the Authors

Lawrence P. Levitt, MD founded the Neurology Division at Lehigh Valley Hospital in Allentown, Pennsylvania, and served as a Dorothy Rider Pool Health Care Trustee. Larry is a graduate of Weill Cornell Medicine and trained at Memorial Sloan Kettering Cancer Center, Bellevue Hospital, and the Peter Bent Brigham Hospital. His previous works include *Neurology for the House Officer* and *Uncommon Wisdom: True Tales of What Our Lives As Doctors Have Taught Us About Love, Faith and Healing*. He was married to the incomparable Eva for sixty-one years and is a father of three and grandfather of six.

Stephanie Smartschan is a journalist by trade turned Jewish nonprofit professional. She got her start working for *The Boston Globe* while a student at Northeastern University and went on to write for *The Cape Cod Times*, covering everything from casinos to courts and nuclear power plants to religion. Her work garnered many regional awards. Stephanie has spent the last thirteen years working in marketing and development for Jewish nonprofits and serves on the boards of local Jewish organizations. She lives in Allentown, Pennsylvania, with her husband Adam and two daughters.

Printed in the USA
CPSIA information can be obtained
at www.ICGtesting.com
CBHW080032270324
5919CB00007B/14

9 781952 352232